Strategic Sales and Strategic Marketing

There is growing evidence that the traditional role of the sales organization in business-to-business marketing is quickly evolving from a tactical, operational function to a strategic capability concerned with the management of critical processes that support business strategy and deliver value to profitable customers. This topic is of major relevance to scholars in both the sales and marketing domains, and this relevance is underlined by the intense interest of managers and companies in how this field is changing.

This collection is a unique gathering of views on the critical issues to be confronted in the strategizing of the sales function, from distinguished scholars from throughout the world. Their focus is on the linkages between strategic marketing and the corollary of strategic sales.

This book was published as a special issue of *Journal of Strategic Marketing*.

Dr Nikala Lane is Associate Professor in Marketing and Strategy at Warwick Business School, the University of Warwick, UK. She was previously at Cardiff University as Senior Research Associate. She has published widely on management, marketing and sales topics and is co-author of *Strategic Customer Management* (Oxford University Press, 2009).

Strategic Sales and Strategic Marketing

Edited by
Nikala Lane

Routledge
Taylor & Francis Group

LONDON AND NEW YORK

First published 2011 by Routledge
2 Park Square, Milton Park, Abingdon, Oxon, OX14 4RN

Simultaneously published in the USA and Canada
by Routledge
711 Third Avenue, New York, NY 10017

Routledge is an imprint of the Taylor & Francis Group, an informa business

This book is a reproduction of *Journal of Strategic Marketing* - Volume 17.3-4. The Publisher requests that those citing this book use the bibliographical details of the journal issue on which the book is based.

Typeset in Times New Roman by Taylor & Francis Books

British Library Cataloguing in Publication Data
A catalogue record for this book is available from the British Library

ISBN13: 978-0-415-61451-1

Disclaimer
The publisher would like to make readers aware that the chapters in this book are referred to as articles as they had been in the special issue. The publisher accepts responsibility for any inconsistencies that may have arisen in the course of preparing this volume for print.

Contents

Strategic sales and strategic marketing

This double-issue of *Journal of Strategic Marketing* (*JSM*) is devoted to the subject of the linkages between sales and strategic marketing, but particularly the way in which these linkages are evolving as scholars and executives take a more strategic view of the traditional sales function and the management of major business-to-business customer relationships.

It seems some considerable time ago now that we started planning a special journal issue concerned with the increasingly strategic role of new types of sales and account management in managing critical relationships with different types of customer, and indeed other types of third party relationships, such as those with alliance and network members and other value chain participants. I am very grateful to the editors of *JSM* for allowing us the time to build what I think will be a very influential set of papers. I am also delighted that they were able to allow us a double issue of the journal, in which to publish our collection of papers.

The underlying rationale for what we have attempted here is the growing evidence that the traditional role of the sales organization in business-to-business marketing is fast evolving from a tactical, operational function to a strategic capability concerned with the management of processes that support business strategy in delivering value to profitable customers. In this sense, there is a case that the much-debated question of the relationship between sales and marketing has been rendered partly obsolete by the importance of the interface between sales and strategy. Related issues pertain to the development of strategic account management models, as an approach to coping with the demands of dominant customers. The topic is of considerable relevance to scholars in both the sales and strategic marketing domains, and this relevance is supported by the intense interest of managers and companies in what is happening in this area.

We suggested to our potential authors that a broad range of topics could be relevant to enhancing our understanding of the new types of sales organizations which are developing: we were interested in the changing role played by sales organizations in business-to-business marketing companies; relatedly process-based models of the contribution of the sales organization to the creation of superior customer value might be insightful; one point of attack could be the evolution in the organizational positioning and form of the customer-facing components of the organization and the development of sales capabilities as a critical resource supporting and influencing business strategy. Possible approaches extended to empirical tests of the effectiveness of sales organizations in implementing business and marketing strategies, and the evaluation of the impact of new organizational forms, like customer business development and strategic account management approaches, on business performance, the effectiveness of organizational linkages between the sales organization and strategic decision making, and tests of the impact of sales capabilities on competitive advantage and business performance.

With this ambitious range of topics we were able to attract an outstanding set of authors to offer their insights into the evolving role of the sales organization in shaping as well as implementing business and marketing strategy. Inevitably, our ambitious target coverage of the field has been only partly achieved. Indeed, one of the exciting implications of the collection is that it helps identify the new work which needs to be done in this area to extend both our conceptual understanding and the value we can offer managers in confronting the practical problems they face in rethinking the role of sales and implementing the organizational changes necessary to support a new strategic sales function.

It is also particularly pleasing to be able to report as Guest Editor that we were successful in attracting contributions to the special issue from some of the most distinguished scholars in this field in the world, but at the same time we were able to balance these with papers from researchers at earlier stages in their research programmes. We believe the originality and potential interest for readers is uniform across the authors and groups represented in the special issue.

The issue starts with an attempt to demonstrate the links between the various contributions and to underline the unique contribution of each.

Nikala Lane
Warwick Business School
nikala.lane@wbs.ac.uk
May 2009

Searching for strategy in sales

Nikala Lane

This issue of the journal contains seven separate contributions to the debate regarding the emergence and characteristics of the strategic sales organization. The papers published here move the strategic sales issue from the generalized prescription of a more strategic approach to sales, to more specific analyses of critical topics: the strategic realignment needed for effective organizational change; the need to capture key account performance as a basis for making strategic choices; the impact of the leaning of operations and lean enterprises spanning value chains on buyer–seller relationships; the need to locate sales ethics in an enterprise-wide ethics system that represents a company's key values and its undertakings to stakeholders; the importance of accommodating marketing/sales interface issues in the transformation process; and, focusing on the processes of strategizing the traditional sales organization for the new type of role it is expected to play.

This volume contains a collection of essays provided by scholars who were challenged to examine the relationships between strategic marketing and the growing strategic role of the sales organization. Our starting point was the observation that the traditional role of the sales organization in business-to-business marketing is fast evolving from a tactical, operational function concerned with the operational implementation of marketing strategies and programmes, to a strategic capability focused on the management of the processes that support business strategy, and which plays a growing role in the shaping of that strategy.

The authors were provided with no direction by the editor as to specific topic or approach to be taken and were allowed complete editorial freedom in how they addressed the central issue and developed insights to take the academic and practical debate forward. The result is a relatively diverse set of contributions, which bring several different insights to the strategic marketing/strategic sales relationship, and yet there are common themes which are worthy of some note.

In the broadest terms, we have grouped the papers in the way discussed below. The grouping and ordering does not imply priorities or relative importance, but a simple and straightforward way of laying out the contributions. Thus, we move from considering the processes of strategic alignment that underpin sales organization transformation (LaForge, Ingram and Cravens) to the driving force of key/strategic account management (Jones, Richards, Halstead and Fu) and the organizational context for value chain

3

collaborations provided by the lean enterprise to which many companies now aspire (Piercy and Rich). A strategic and enterprise-wide approach to ethics in sales (Ferrell and Ferrell) provides an important structure for incorporating in our thinking a critical moral dimension. Two contributions return to the marketing/sales interface as one of the topics which once again becomes significant in the context of an important organizational transformation (Malshe; Fitzhugh and Lane). Finally, we examine the strategizing of the sales organization in terms of the types of changes which are unfolding, how they can be managed and the research opportunities they provide for scholars (Lane and Piercy).

In overview, the contribution of each piece to the general debate can be identified as follows.

Strategic alignment

While it is common to discuss the alignment (and by implication realignment) of sales processes with market change, LaForge et al. develop a detailed and compelling framework for identifying the types of alignment underpinning the strategic sales organization, their logic and rationale and the management challenges faced in achieving this kind of fundamental organizational change in developing superior customer value offers.

Two major contributions stand out from this paper. First, the authors provide a novel integrative model which compares sales organization transformation characteristics (sales organization strategy and sales management practice) to firm transformation. Their logic is that as the firm creates market orientation to focus efforts on superior customer value, this leads to a focus on customer relationship management and strategic relationships, a shift from emphasis on structure to one on process, promoting marketing and sales cooperation and the determination of new metrics based on the transformation. Their model links each aspect of firm-level transformation to related changes in sales organization strategy and sales management practice, as a basis for developmental action by management.

Second, and most particularly, the development of their model rests on the identification and evaluation of the underlying interfaces where strategic alignment is a priority. Their view of sales organization strategy examines alignment in terms of: the link between market orientation and customer-oriented selling; the impact of strategic relationships (e.g. with major customers) on sales and selling strategy (in terms of customer segmentation, relationship selling, sales channel strategy); the need to map process structures onto sales processes and vice versa; the marketing/sales relationship; and, the need to change sales organization metrics to match those used by the firm and the marketing function. Correspondingly, LaForge et al. identify the alignment priorities for sales management practice: customer-oriented selling and sales management alignment; sales strategy and sales management alignment; sales process and sales management alignment; marketing and sales relationship alignment with sales management; and alignment between sales organization strategy metrics and sales management practice. This conceptualization provides a rationale for sales organization transformation management imperatives and a framework identifying several interesting research opportunities.

Importantly, in addition to their compelling models of transformation and alignment interfaces, the LaForge et al. rationale also provides us with several links to other contributions.

Key/strategic account relationships and the lean enterprise

The rationale for emphasizing strategic alignment is related among other factors to the impact of strategic relationships with major customers, and to firm-level transformation. The next two papers in our collection examine in more detail important aspects of these shaping forces: key account management and the implications of the lean enterprise. Both papers address in different ways the essentially cross-functional processes that develop to handle complex relationships with major customers.

Jones et al. have developed a strategic framework for key account performance. The urgency and importance of developing valid and diagnostically useful performance criteria for key or strategic account relationships is underlined by the choices companies face in how they realign processes around such customers. In these terms the key account issue becomes a matter of firm-level investment (or disinvestment) based on the chosen criteria of performance.

The Jones et al. conceptualization introduces a strategic framework for key account management drawing on the strategic marketing theories of relationship marketing, key account management and customer equity. Their framework uses three drivers of customer equity (value equity, brand equity and relationship equity) to examine both important relational outcomes (relationship commitment and trust), and financial performance outcomes (profitability and share of customer spend), which are produced by the strategic decisions made in key account programmes.

Importantly, the Jones et al. framework provides a mechanism for directly relating key account performance to the strategic choices that the firm makes in dealing with key accounts. Their framework has a four-part structure: the strategic decisions made in the key account programme; resulting improvements in value equity, brand equity and relationship equity; producing greater relationship commitment and trust; ultimately driving the performance of the key account in profitability and share of spend. They place emphasis on the linkage between marketing strategy choices and the growth of value, brand and relationship equity to make the link between strategic marketing choices and key account performance fully explicit.

This contribution relates both to the search for appropriate process alignment strategies discussed by LaForge et al., but also to the major questions which have been raised regarding the potentially unequal sharing of benefits between sellers and their key accounts (see, for example, Fink, Edelman, & Hatten, 2007). The link between marketing strategy and key account performance is emerging as a critical firm-level issue in making choices about transformation investment.

Piercy and Rich also draw attention to the essentially cross-functional nature of the processes surrounding relationships with customers and suppliers as value chain partners. Their focus is on the lean enterprise, as it has become a common model in approaching operations and manufacturing management in many European and US businesses. The parallel with the key account management issue is that central to the lean operation is a significant shift in the management of supplier relationships, and particularly the shift from transactional, cost-based buying to long-term collaborative partnerships. The central argument made by Piercy and Rich is that the nature of purchasing and sourcing in the lean organization presents unique challenges for the seller, which are not yet fully recognized. They underline the problems for the traditionally organized sales operation in coping with the requirements of lean customers for complete transparency across supplying organizations and their focus on organizational capability rather than simply cost. Indeed, one implication of selling to the lean organization is the mandate for the seller to adopt lean strategies and organizational designs. The pressure to become lean adds a further dimension to the strategic realignment of processes in the transforming sales organization and the strategic choices in investments with value chain partners (key accounts).

They describe a process whereby the effects of lean change pull the sales force away from traditional production/sales-push approaches (selling existing products to customers based on discounting), towards offering bespoke services that the buying customer wants and needs. This leads to an additional and powerful force for sales force transformation. While the Piercy and Rich contribution is developed from an operations and supply chain perspective, their argument resonates with the issues of market orientation and transformation in buyer–seller relationships. Importantly, from a cross-functional perspective, they point to the need for the lean sales force.

Piercy and Rich produce case study evidence to identify the changing role and requirements for sales under lean sourcing. Their findings point to: the changing role of price and the decline of price-based competition; greater product customization; higher service provision; managing orders to avoid holding stock in the supply chain; working with internal departments to change working practices; and, the sales organization playing a greater role in education and information sharing as opposed to traditional adversarial and low-trust exchanges sometimes found in traditional sales practices. Perhaps the strongest message from the Piercy and Rich contribution is underlining cross-functional interests in buyer–seller relationship management and the implications of active cross-functionality for a new type of sales organization.

An ethical dimension becomes an imperative

The recurring themes of market orientation and cross-functional process underpinning the strategic sales organization are further reinforced in the Ferrell and Ferrell appraisal of sales ethics in an enterprise-wide stakeholder approach. Their position is, in fact, that a strategic stakeholder orientation goes beyond market orientation, and customer orientation to provide the foundation for an organizational ethical culture and an ethical sales sub-culture.

The underlying logic for this approach is that strategic sales leadership built on an ethical organizational culture contributes to ethical decision making and plays a strong role in building transparency and trust with stakeholders. Their framework seeks to provide a strategic approach to developing and sustaining an enterprise-wide perspective that includes sales ethics. Their approach uses a stakeholder framework (including the needs of employees, suppliers, regulators, special interest groups, communities and the media) to position sales in a strategic role, participating in the development and implementation of ethical marketing practice. Their strategic approach to ethics develops a process for addressing stakeholder issues, including: creating a strategic focus on stakeholders, risk tolerance and culture; developing guidelines and boundaries for acceptable practices; and, creating mechanisms for continuous improvement. In this approach, the strategic sales organization needs to consider enterprise-wide stakeholders, to identify and prioritize their concerns and to gather information to respond to significant individuals, groups and communities.

Their concern is that frequently sales has operated in a situation where role and rewards are based on a single, financial criterion, so that incentives for performance obscure stakeholder perspectives. Instead, they look for a corporate culture that establishes appropriate norms and values to establish boundaries for activities, including compliance, core practices, a commitment to excel and voluntary contributions to integrity. Implementation of their approach is facilitated by a triple bottom-line concept, incorporating economic, environmental and social factors.

The Ferrell and Ferrell contribution is especially timely at a point when as a result of corporate scandals, public trust in business and the integrity of executives appears at an all-time low (see, for example, Milne, 2009). It is increasingly the case that ethical standards provide a major criterion determining whether a buyer–seller relationship is attractive to both parties, and how well it can function if there are major divisions in values and ethical norms between the parties. There are also growing concerns that some key/strategic account relationships may be founded on principles of questionable ethical standing (Piercy & Lane, 2007). This point resonates with the earlier arguments regarding strategic alignment between buyer and seller and the attractiveness of key accounts, but adds an additional and critical dimension to this debate. They make the telling point that ethics is an enterprise-wide issue in which sales plays a critical role, rather than simply mandating compliance to codes of 'fair practice' from those in selling roles.

The sales/marketing interface dilemma returns to the agenda

We have two contributions providing perspectives on the marketing/sales interface in the context of the strategic sales organization transformation. Malshe examines the transformation challenges and facilitators in the marketing/sales interface, while Fitzhugh and Lane examine collaboration between marketing and sales and the links to market orientation and business performance.

Malshe's perspective is that as companies adopt and develop sales organizations with more strategic characteristics, then they need to pay attention to the intra-organizational factors that may facilitate or challenge this transformation. He uses qualitative executive interview data to examine the role-related and process-related factors that may either facilitate or challenge the organizational change underpinning the new approach to sales. His logic is that a mismatch in the role perceptions between the functions of marketing and sales may undermine effective organizational realignment around strategic imperatives, suggesting that the emergence of the strategic sales organization may require marketing and sales personnel to rethink their traditional strategy creation and implementation processes.

Malshe's research addresses two fundamental questions associated with these dilemmas: what are the similarities and differences between sales and marketing in their expectations of the role each function should play in the strategy process; and how will these differences in role expectations create facilitators or challenges for the strategic sales organization.

His findings suggest that marketing executives see themselves as the 'strategic hub' with the desire to maintain key strategy decision makers, not heavily involved in tactical activities. They saw the sales organization primarily as an implementation capability. Sales executives, on the other hand, viewed their role as strategic and emphasized acting as customer advocate in the firm. They did not view themselves as purely implementers of strategy, but as strategic players. Salespeople saw marketers as removed from reality, providing inadequate sales support and lacking customer–contact. These findings suggest both facilitators and challenges for organizational change.

Malshe's study provides a detailed comparison of role expectations across the marketing/sales interface, and provides a dramatic contrast between how marketing and sales personnel view themselves and how they are viewed by their counterparts. He starts to uncover, in a way neglected in the prior literature, guidance regarding what the emergence of the strategic sales organization entails for the existing and traditional sales and marketing functions.

The second piece addressing marketing/sales interface issues is provided by Fitzhugh and Lane. Their study examines whether improving collaboration between sales and marketing provides benefits in terms of stronger market orientation and higher business performance. They also consider the link between market intelligence systems and management attitudes and market orientation. Their results confirm that collaboration between marketing and sales has a positive and significant impact on market orientation and business performance.

Their emphasis on market orientation in this context continues the importance of this theme. Interestingly, their study examines not integration of the two functions (since they perform quite different activities) but collaboration across organizational divisions. They focus attention on organizational factors which may support or undermine this type of inter-functional collaboration: internal competition, different goals and metrics and time horizons – leading to distrust and conflict.

The importance of this theme to the strategic sales organization is that in reality companies rarely start with a clean sheet of paper when realigning. Reality is represented by the organizational status quo, and all that is implied in terms of resource and process control. The better understood is the relationship between the sales and marketing functions, the more likely that appropriate transformation policies can be developed by management.

Processes of strategizing the sales organization

The last paper in the collection is provided by Lane and Piercy, and it offers a managerial structure for addressing the factors involved in the development of the strategic sales organization. This framework relates to several of the themes raised by the earlier contributions. It aims to provide an integrated model of the areas to be addressed in developing and enhancing the effectiveness of the strategic sales organization.

The model suggests five areas closely related to the realignment of the sales role in the organizations: the involvement of sales in strategy development rather than simply implementation; the development of enhanced market and customer intelligence systems to better inform business strategy decisions and provide the basis for added-value for customers; the integration of company resources around meeting customer priorities; the internal marketing of customers to employees and managers inside the company; and the development of new sales infrastructure to better align sales processes and structure with business strategy.

In addition, the model suggests four further, broader areas for management attention in achieving the transformation of the sales organization. These identify as priorities: providing leadership and inspiration within the company; exerting influence over corporate decisions and choices; developing integrity in terms both of ethical standards and corporate social responsibility initiatives that impact on customer relationships; and, adopting an international perspective that looks past national boundaries to accommodate globalizing customers and new sources of competition.

Common themes and research directions

Perhaps one of the most striking features shared by the contributions to this issue is the degree to which the authors address very tangible issues, which are both of practical significance to executives, but also provide a framework for useful and insightful research endeavours. The concept of the strategic sales organization is not new. Benson Shapiro and his colleagues underlined the concept and its appeal in the late 1990s (see, for example, Shapiro, Slywotski, & Doyle, 1998) and continue to pursue their work. Nonetheless, our contributions turn from the general prescriptive concept of the strategic sales organization to tease out the particulars of how such a structure and set of processes can operate in practice, and the related research agenda which starts to emerge from this specificity. Importantly, this process of focus emphasizes the links between the strategic sales organization and strategic marketing.

The papers reflect a view that fundamental change in the market and in customer demands and expectations provides a basis for driving important organizational change. Nonetheless, it is clear from several of the commentaries that this transformation will depend for its effectiveness on considerable efforts at company-wide realignment of processes and structures, and particularly careful attention to managing the marketing/sales interface and how this may operate in a reinvented organization.

There is a strong theme running through the papers emphasizing cross-functionality – suggesting that the strategic sales organization will occupy a domain quite different to that of the conventional sales department, and is likely to play a far greater role within the seller organization and operate across functions than has been the case in the traditional sales role. Strong and effective links to operations, supply chain, marketing and other specialist groups are likely to be key to effectiveness in managing strategic relationships with customers.

A further critical element of the new environment for the reinvented sales organization is provided by the imperative of undertaking and openly displaying high ethical standards in dealing with others. While the moral mandate has always been present, the growing demands for integrity and corporate responsibility cannot be ignored in developing a strategic sales organization.

Lastly, and perhaps the strongest link between the papers is their shared emphasis on market orientation. This perhaps demonstrates most powerfully the link between strategic developments in the sales organization and the domain of strategic marketing. The authors suggest variously that the strategic sales organization represents the extension and enhancement of a company's market orientation, is a driver of transformation effectiveness and may be a consequence of the organizational realignment being considered. While the exact ordering of the constructs remains an untested empirical issue, what is clear in the views of our authors is that market orientation and the transformation of the traditional sales organization are closely related issues.

References

Fink, R.C., Edelman, L.F., & Hatten, K.J. (2007). Supplier performance improvements in relational exchanges. *Journal of Business and Industrial Marketing, 22*(1), 29–40.

Milne, R. (2009, April 14). How business became bogeyman. *Financial Times*, p. 6.

Piercy, N.F., & Lane, N. (2007). Ethical and moral dimensions associated with strategic relationships between business-to-business buyers and sellers. *Journal of Business Ethics, 72*, 87–102.

Shapiro, B.P., Slywotsky, A.J., & Doyle, S.X. (1998). *Strategic sales management: A boardroom issue*. Harvard Business School Note 9-595-018. Boston, MA: Harvard Business School.

Strategic alignment for sales organization transformation

Raymond W. LaForge, Thomas N. Ingram and David W. Cravens

The highly competitive, turbulent business environment calls for the creation and delivery of superior customer value. In order to meet customer expectations and deliver superior value, many firms are undergoing significant transformations by developing a market orientation, building strategic relationships, improving processes and structures, enhancing the relationship between the marketing and sales functions, and developing appropriate new metrics. This paper addresses the crucial role of the sales organization and the importance of strategic alignment to the success of firm and sales organization transformations. Key alignment linkages between firm transformation strategy, sales organization strategy, and sales management practice are discussed in the context of delivering superior customer value. Sales organization implications and research directions are discussed.

Many companies are undergoing a strategic transformation to compete effectively in a turbulent business environment. Increasingly, the success of these efforts is dependent upon significant transformations within a firm's sales organization. The driving force for the firm and sales organization transformation is to deliver superior customer value. Important sales organization changes might include (Piercy & Lane, 2005):

- Involvement in strategic decision making at the corporate and business strategy levels.
- Market sensing and interpretation.
- Building cross-functional collaborative relationships.
- Serving as the customer's advocate inside the organization.

Sales organizations need to develop and implement changes that strategically align the sales organization with the company's business and marketing strategies to create a more customer-focused sales organization with the emphasis placed on the sales organization rather than the salesperson (Sheth & Sharma, 2008). The key linkages that must be aligned for sales organizations to be successful in their transformation efforts are:

- Sales organization strategy changes need to be aligned with the firm's transformational efforts.
- Sales management practice must be aligned with sales organization strategy changes.
- Firm and sales organization transformations must be aligned with customer needs to create and deliver superior customer value.

Our objective is to discuss the critical role of the sales organization in translating business and marketing strategy changes into the creation and delivery of superior value to priority customers. We begin with an examination of several important trends that are precipitating the need for strategic transformations in many firms and the important elements in these strategic transformations. Then, we discuss the key linkages between firm transformation efforts and the alignment of sales organization strategy and sales management practice with a focus on ensuring that all efforts are aligned with customer needs. Finally, we offer sales organization implications and future research directions.

Competitive and turbulent business environment

Businesses around the world are encountering an array of rapid changes. We examine several demanding challenges and discuss how these challenges create the need for firms and sales organizations to emphasize the creation and delivery of superior customer value.

Escalating customer expectations

Because of increasing expectations, building strong relationships with customers is a high priority strategic initiative for companies around the world. In an international study, some 1000 executives rated customer relationship management and strategic planning highest among 10 priority strategic actions for improving business performance (*The Economist*, 2005). Rapid global expansion and the challenge of gaining a strong competitive position highlight the importance of changing a firm's strategies to meet the rising expectations of customers and to increase business performance.

Services as the dominant focus

A significant change in the conceptualization of services is underway. Instead of the traditional view of tangible goods versus intangible services, a transformation has been proposed that this distinction should be replaced by a service-centered logic, comprised of both goods and services which deliver value to customers (Vargo & Lusch, 2004). The core challenge is understanding the composition of the value offering being made to customers. This shift in perspective away from a focus on goods toward service is rapidly gaining support from academics and executives: 'A service-centered view of exchange implies customized offerings to better fit customers' needs and identifying firm resources – both internal and external – to better satisfy the needs of customers' (Sheth & Sharma, 2008, p. 262). Related developments include the shift toward the exchange of intangibles, specialized skills, knowledge, and processes, as well as the co-creation of value between buyers and sellers.

The importance of information technology

Information technology (IT) will continue to have a major impact on business research and practice: 'Advances in IT have reshaped all aspects of marketing, but the impacts on buyer–seller relationships in business markets are especially dramatic' (Hunter & Perreault, 2007, p. 16). A major challenge is to avoid allowing technology to dominate strategic thought and action. This has been a problem in more than a few strategic customer relationship management initiatives. IT is clearly an essential component of business, marketing, and sales organization strategies but should not direct these important organizational processes. New developments in IT can help firms implement strategic transformation initiatives effectively and efficiently.

Global perspective

The competitive and turbulent business environment is increasingly global in scope. Senior marketing and sales executives face demanding challenges in managing their businesses, marketing efforts, and sales organizations, which are competing in other countries (Cravens, Piercy, & Low, 2006). No matter how narrow an organization's market scope, understanding global markets and competitive space is important, since competitive threats may develop throughout the world (Cravens, 2006). Superior customer value delivery needs a global perspective to identify high-value customers and to facilitate customer relationship management across national boundaries.

Strategic thinking and organizational change

Markets are increasingly complex and hyper-competitive (Cravens, 2006). Excess capacities are significantly modifying opportunities and competitive space. While there are many influences creating the importance of strategic thinking for changing markets, disruptive innovation (simpler, more convenient products), commoditization of products (goods and services), value driven segmentation, and creation of new market space are particularly relevant. The logic of structure following strategy is widely acknowledged by organizational design authorities (Roberts, 2004). But design is becoming more complex due to emerging changes from hierarchical structures to core processes, and the need to develop skills to gain better cross-functional cooperation across business functions.

Superior customer value mandate

The demanding challenges confronting companies around the world clearly indicate the need for strategic transformation initiatives by firms and sales organizations to create superior customer value. The success of these initiatives requires close alignment between the firm and sales organization and between sales organization strategy and sales management practice. All transformation efforts must also be aligned with the needs of customers. Table 1 presents the key alignment linkages we will discuss.

Hewlett-Packard (H-P) provides a recent example of the key role of the sales organization in a firm transformation, as well as the critical linkages that require alignment for the success of firm and sales organization transformations (Tam, 2006). H-P's newly appointed CEO initiated the transformation process by obtaining responses from 400 B-2-B customers concerning their needs and experiences with H-P. Based on this customer information, H-P began the process of transforming the firm into a market-oriented company focused on creating and delivering superior value to customers. Changes at the firm level triggered major alterations of H-P's sales organization strategy and sales management practice. Sales organization strategy changes included an emphasis on meeting the specific needs of different B2B customers. More salespeople were added and each salesperson was assigned

Table 1. Sales organization transformation alignment.

FIRM TRANSFORMATION	Create market orientation to focus firm efforts on superior customer value	⇑	Focus on customer relationship management and external and internal strategic relationships	⇑	Shift from structure emphasis to firm processes	⇑	Promote marketing and sales cooperation	⇑	Determine new metrics based on transformation strategy
SALES ORGANIZATION TRANSFORMATION									
Sales Organization Strategy	Emphasize customer-oriented selling to focus salespeople on co-creating value with customers		Craft sales strategies for strategic accounts and customer segments and external and internal strategic relationships		Develop sales processes for strategic accounts and customer segments		Coordinate marketing and sales efforts in prospecting and in the development of sales support materials		Include more long-term and customer-oriented metrics
Sales Management Practice	Establish culture, climate, socialization, and sales management activities to promote customer-oriented selling		Devise sales organization structure and sales management activities to support sales strategies		Involve field sales managers in developing sales processes and use sales processes as basis for leading and managing salespeople		Proactive efforts by sales managers to work closely with marketing		Use new metrics in salesperson performance and development efforts

fewer customers and expected to develop closer relationships with them. Sales management changes were widespread. The sales organization structure was revamped to remove several management layers and to establish a product-specialized sales organization. Sales software was standardized and new training programs developed and implemented. The alignment of the firm and sales organization transformation efforts with customers needs produced significant improvement in H-P's performance.

Strategic transformation of the firm

The strategic transformation of a firm might encompass a variety of activities. Figure 1 presents important elements in many firm strategic transformations. The specific changes made by a particular firm depend upon its unique situation.

Market orientation

Market orientation (MO) is an organization-wide perspective that positions the customer at the center of a company's total operations: 'A business is market-oriented when its culture is systematically and entirely committed to the continuous creation of superior customer value' (Slater & Narver, 1994, p. 23). The MO construct consists of both a culture and a process. Becoming market oriented requires superior organizational capabilities in understanding and satisfying customers (Day, 1990). Successfully implementing the process demands the involvement of all the members of the organization. Importantly, the focus is 'market' and customers rather than the 'marketing' function.

MO is very relevant to our strategic alignment framework because the construct is closely linked to achieving superior customer value. Moreover, there is extensive empirical support of a positive relationship between MO and business performance (Deshpandé & Farley, 2004; Kirca, Jayachandran, & Bearden, 2005; Verhoef & Leeflang, 2008).

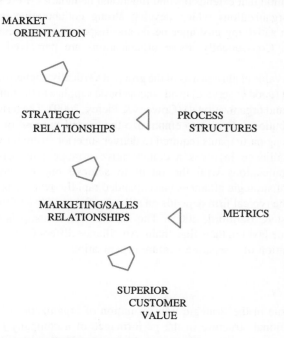

Figure 1.   Strategic transformation process of the organization.

In their meta-analysis, Kirca et al. (2005) found that the positive MO and performance relationship is stronger in their samples of manufacturing firms compared to service providers, although significant in both groups. The stronger results were also found in low power-distance and uncertainty-avoidance cultures.

We propose that becoming market oriented is an essential part of strategic transformation of the organization. Kirca et al. (2005) found that top management emphasis on MO, interdepartmental connectedness, and market-based reward systems were relevant antecedents of MO. These findings have important implications for organizational implementation of MO, implying that top management plays a pivotal role, cross-functional cooperation is beneficial, and employee rewards linked to customers enhance the MO process. Thus, activating the antecedents appears to be essential in becoming market oriented.

Strategic relationships

Strategic relationships among suppliers, producers, distribution (value chain) channel organizations, and customers (end-users and intermediate customers) have important implications for a company. Relationships may be formed to reach markets, improve customer value offerings, reduce risk, share distinctive skills, develop collaborative relationships with customers, and access needed resources. Strategic relationships are an important dimension in the strategic transformation of the firm. Relationships within the organization, value chain relationships, and strategic alliances are particularly relevant.

Internal organizational partnering is essential in achieving superior customer value. Relationships may develop across business units, departments, and specific employees. The relationship objective is to move beyond specialization toward cooperation across functions in areas such as research and development, marketing, sales, purchasing, finance, and operations (Cravens & Piercy, 2009). Central to the relationship process is fostering strong internal collaboration that extends beyond functional boundaries. Research findings support the logic that organizations which develop strong collaborative internal relationships perform better in satisfying customer needs and responding to special customer requests (Wilding, 2006). Consequently, these organizations are perceived more favorably by their customers.

A company's value chain consists of the group of vertically aligned organizations that add value to a product (good or service) in advancing basic supplies to the finished product for end users (consumer and organizational) (Cravens & Piercy, 2009). The term *value chain* is used to identify distribution activities to emphasize the central purpose of the process and the relationships among participants required to deliver superior customer value.

A strategic alliance involves a collaborative arrangement between two or more independent organizations with the intent to achieve one or more shared strategic objectives. Use of strategic alliances has expanded rapidly over the last two decades. One estimate is that the typical firm depends on alliances for 15–20% of total revenues, assets, or income (Ernst & Bamford, 2005). The alliance relationship is horizontal with the partner at the same level in the value chain. An alliance differs from a joint venture in that there is no formation of a separate venture organization.

Process structures

An important issue in the strategic transformation of organizations is recognition of the role of organizational structure in the performance of a company in responding to the requirements of new strategies (Cravens & Piercy, 2009). Traditional vertical hierarchies create major hurdles in strategic transformation of companies. Important responses to needed structural changes are reduction in the number of organizational levels and development of process structures.

A core challenge in making organizational design changes is shifting emphasis from structure to managing organizational processes, and moving from traditional structure to horizontal designs. Not surprisingly, the organizational transition processes have been very slow. Few, if any, organizations have developed horizontal structures. Most re-designs have coupled fewer levels of functional structures with process overlays.

In the twenty-first century major priority has been placed by strategy authorities on the need for companies to adopt process structures (e.g. Day, 1994; Webster, 1997). Nonetheless, the rigidity of functional structures has been difficult to change, particularly in large companies. The impacts of the organizational changes include fewer levels and fewer managers, greater emphasis on the use of cross-functional teams, and increased focus on distinctive capabilities and delivery of superior customer value (Cravens, 2006).

One important characteristic of process-type structures is the development of cross-functional teams:

> Teams are organized around three core processes: the consumer management team, replacing the brand management function, is responsible for customer segments; customer process teams, replacing the sales function, serve the retail accounts; and the supply management team, absorbing the logistics function, ensures on-time delivery to retailers. There is also a strategic integration team, to develop effective overall strategies and coordinate the teams. Although this team relies on deep understanding of the market, it might not be in the marketing function. While functions remain, their roles are to coordinate activities across teams to ensure that shared learning takes place, to acquire and nurture specialized skills, to deploy specialists to the cross-functional process teams, and to achieve scale economies. (Day, 1997, p. 72)

Transition to a process orientation requires capabilities in negotiation, conflict resolution, relationship management, communication, and team building (Webster, 1997). Cross-functional skills are essential in new product planning, value chain coordination, customer relationship management, and strategic alliances. Importantly, these are new skills for managers and professionals experienced in functional organizations.

As discussed in previous sections, companies are moving toward closer linkages with their markets because of changes in their business and marketing strategies and escalating customer expectations. Business focus is shifting from products to markets and market segments. The alignment process appears to be moving through three stages of transition based on research findings: (1) improving alignment via informal lateral integration; (2) adopting integrating mechanisms using key account or market segment managers; and (3) complete customer alignment with customer-based units at the front of the organization or segment focused matrix structures (Day, 2005). Few, if any, organizations have advanced to the third step.

Marketing and sales relationships

The marketing and sales functions in the organization are very relevant in the process of creation and delivery of superior customer value. We know that positioning strategy consists of integrated product, distribution, pricing, and promotion strategies designed to favorably position a company or business unit with targeted end-user customers. The marketing and sales functions are responsible for different objectives and activities, yet a strong positive relationship is essential in delivering superior customer value. Importantly, because the nature of selling is changing, there is an increasing need for greater coordination between sales and marketing (Cespedes, 1995). Marketing and sales are organized as separate functions and departments in many companies, and conflict rather than collaboration is typical (Workman, Homburg, & Gruner, 1998): 'The relationship between the sales and marketing functions has persisted as one of the major sources of organizational conflict' (Webster, 1997, p. 45).

Surprisingly, the marketing and sales relationship has received very limited research attention. A recent study highlights the importance of the relationship. The researchers investigated the different thought worlds that are characteristic of each function (Homburg & Jensen, 2007), and identified the likely taxonomies which describe most marketing and sales relationships (Homburg, Jensen, & Krohmer, 2008). However, the study findings are somewhat inconsistent. Marketing thought leaders have expressed concerns about marketing and sales conflict and propose the need for increased collaboration between the two functions (Kotler, Rackham, & Krishnaswamy, 2006). There is strong conceptual logic supporting the importance of collaboration between marketing and sales in achieving superior customer value. Missing from marketing and sales research findings is identification of promising antecedents of favorable collaboration relationships between the two functions.

Metrics

Marketing metrics are receiving significant attention by academics and executives who are stimulated by concerns about how to measure marketing performance and link it with business performance (O'Sullivan & Abela, 2007). Metrics are designated a top priority research issue by the Marketing Science Institute. Measures may be developed to evaluate position relative to competition, effectiveness with the customer and customer value, marketing program effectiveness, and financial performance (Ferris, Bendle, Pfeifer, & Reibstein, 2006). Authorities in marketing metrics caution against relying on a single measure (Ambler & Roberts, 2006; Lehmann, 2004). Eight to 10 metrics are recommended for a large firm with less for a smaller business.

A core consideration is deciding which metrics to use. Several guidelines are proposed: (1) measure performance relative to strategy; (2) monitor performance relative to both competitors and customers; (3) track performance over time; and (4) analyze performance to examine the impact of different strategy components being changed (Clark, 2001). An increasingly important metrics issue is developing a marketing dashboard to provide top level management with a condensed set of key measures to communicate and evaluate the firm's marketing performance (Ferris et al., 2006).

The result of this process for a specific firm is the development of specific changes desired to transform the firm in a manner that will allow it to create and deliver superior customer value. The success of the transformation requires close alignment with the sales organization. Specific linkages between the sales organization strategy and sales management practice are especially important.

Strategic transformation of the sales organization

An executive in corporate marketing at a large industrial firm commented to the authors:

> We have an effective process for developing business and marketing strategies, but then we throw these strategies over the wall and tell salespeople to go sell. There is a clear need to have an effective strategy to implement our business and marketing strategies.

This firm initiated a strategic transformation process that focused on creating a world-class sales organization. Initial efforts emphasized the alignment of sales organization strategy with changes in business and marketing strategies. The sales management practices were altered to implement the sales organization strategy successfully.

As indicated in Table 1, it is important to transform the sales organization in a manner that is aligned with the firm's transformation efforts and the needs of customers. Effective alignment of the firm and sales organization focused on creating and delivering superior customer value is the essence of our conceptual logic and approach. We now examine sales organization strategy and sales management practice because these areas need to be aligned internally to successfully transform a sales organization.

Sales organization strategy alignment

Although sales organization strategy might be conceptualized in different ways, we examine the specific links between the key elements in a firm transformation (see Figure 1) and specific aspects of sales organization strategy.

Market orientation–customer-oriented selling alignment

One key alignment linkage is between a market orientation at the company level and customer-oriented selling at the sales organization level. Customer-oriented selling has been defined in various ways, but all definitions emphasize a focus on satisfying the needs of customers as a basis for developing long-term customer relationships (Schwepker, 2003) with three key elements highlighted: diagnosing and determining customer needs; helping customers make sound purchasing decisions; and avoiding the use of deceptive, manipulative, and high-pressure sales tactics (Saxe & Weitz, 1982). Recently, Ingram, LaForge, Avila, Schwepker, and Williams (2009) identified another key role of customer-oriented salespeople, in which salespeople act as customer value agents. In this role, salespeople play an active part in creating, communicating, delivering, and continually increasing customer value. Salespeople who serve as customer value agents do more than communicate value; they are actively involved in co-creating value with customers over an extended time horizon.

Research suggests important relationships between adaptive selling and customer-oriented selling, and between customer-oriented selling and salesperson performance and job satisfaction (Franke & Park, 2006). Customer-oriented selling can be conceptualized as part of the culture of a sales organization as well as the specific behaviors of salespeople during their interactions with customers (Cross, Brashear, Rigdon, & Bellenger, 2007). Customer-oriented selling has been linked positively to a number of important outcomes, including higher levels of customer satisfaction with the selling firm (Humphreys & Williams, 1996), strength of long-term customer relationships (Schultz & Good, 2000), and the creation of superior customer value (Guenzi & Troilo, 2007).

HR Chally (2007) and Stevens and Kinni (2007) studied 80,000 business buyers served by 210,000 salespeople in 15 industries over a 14-year time period to determine what buyers typically define as value. The study results suggest that business buyers value sales organizations that understand their business, create and deliver applications that solve their problems, act as customer advocates, are readily accessible, and are a source of innovative ideas. These activities provide important guidelines for sales organizations in establishing customer-oriented selling as a key linkage between a firm's overall market orientation and its specific selling orientation interacting with and creating superior value for customers.

Strategic relationships–sales strategy alignment

The importance of strategic relationships and customer relationship management is acknowledged widely and was discussed earlier. Rapidly escalating customer demands for innovation and superior value in combination with altered types of relationships with suppliers are creating the need for important changes in the nature and scope of the traditional sales organization (Piercy & Lane, 2005). Sales organizations need to craft a sales strategy to guide sales efforts with individual customers or customer segments. The sales strategy should balance the buyer's relationship perspective as well the potential profitability expectations of serving different customer groups in different ways.

Many business buyers have developed formal supplier relationship management (SRM) or supplier sourcing strategies to guide their desired relationships with suppliers (Kocabasoglu & Suresh, 2006). Although these approaches differ across companies, one popular approach is for organizational purchasers to segment suppliers into different groups based on the strategic importance of each supplier and the availability of substitute suppliers (Page, 2006). Using high and low evaluations for each dimension produces four supplier segments: strategic suppliers; preferred suppliers; manage risk suppliers; and commodity suppliers. The potential for developing close relationships with customers depends largely on where a buyer classifies a particular seller. The best opportunity for long-term customer relationships is for strategic suppliers with little relationship possibilities for commodity suppliers. Thus, the sourcing strategy of business buyers has an important impact on sales strategy development.

The creation of specific sales strategies for customers or customer segments has been suggested as an extremely important, but often neglected, activity for sales organizations (Ingram, LaForge, & Leigh, 2002). Sales strategies provide the opportunity to align selling efforts with the needs of customers and as a way to implement business and marketing strategies effectively. Our conceptualization of sales strategy includes customer segmentation and prioritization, relationship strategies and sales processes, and the use of multiple sales channels (Ingram et al., 2009).

Customer segmentation

The cornerstone of an effective sales strategy is to segment and prioritize customer segments. The prioritization of accounts provides a way to achieve higher average customer profitability and a higher return on sales, because it improves relationships with the most important customers, does not affect relationships with less important customers, and reduces marketing and sales costs (Homburg, Droll, & Totzek, 2008). Strategic accounts (also called key accounts or major accounts) are large, complex, and the most important customers that are typically considered separately outside this segmentation process. Most sales organizations are likely to have three to five customer segments that differ in importance to the sales organization and require different types of sales attention and selling effort.

Relationship selling

Specific relationship strategies and sales processes are determined for each customer segment. For example, strategic partnership relationships and customized sales processes might be designed for strategic accounts and the most important customer segments. Transaction relationships with basic sales processes are often the only way to profitably serve the least important customer segments. Between these two extremes are customer segments that vary in terms of importance to the firm and the type of sales strategy required to serve them profitably. The key challenge is to align the type of relationship and sales process with each customer segment in a way that meets the needs of customers, but in a cost-effective manner.

Sales channel strategy

The final element of a sales strategy is the sales channel strategy. The potential use of multiple sales channels allows the sales organization to balance customer needs with the costs of serving customers. This applies to strategic accounts and each different customer segment and for sales activities within each segment. Typically, each strategic account and customer segment in a firm's sales strategy will be served by a different core sales channel. Strategic accounts and the most important customers and segments normally receive the most expensive selling attention from multi-functional sales teams, such as global account management or strategic account management teams. The least important customer segments are not likely to receive personal selling attention, but be served through electronic interaction, direct mail, or telemarketing efforts. Customers in segments between these extremes usually are served by field salespeople, but the salespeople may be from the firm, distributors, or manufacturer's representatives. The linkage between the core selling channel and the appropriate customer segment must also be aligned with the type of relationship and sales process for the customer segment.

In addition to a core sales channel for each customer segment, sales organizations can use different sales channels for different sales process activities within each customer segment. The basic guideline is to use the most cost-effective sales channel for each activity in the sales process. For example, even though a firm's salespeople are the core sales channel for a customer segment, salespeople do not have to perform all of the sales process activities. Direct mail might be used to generate leads, telemarketers qualify and prioritize the leads into prospects, outside salespeople create the relationship, and inside salespeople maintain the relationships with customers. Even though field salespeople are the core sales channel in this example, many sales process activities can be performed effectively, but at a cost much lower than that for field salespeople.

The sales strategy focuses on relationships with customers. But, as discussed earlier, internal relationships and relationships within the value chain and with strategic alliance partners are also very important. This is especially relevant when sales organizations employ multiple sales channels to interact with different customers. PepsiCo Inc. is an interesting example of the effective use of these types of strategic relationships in the beverage division of a company. Pepsi's US field sales organization is deployed into geographical regions, each headed by a vice president. Pepsi is positioned in a value chain comprised of soft-drink bottlers, end-user and intermediate customers (e.g. fast food chains, supermarket chains), and internal relationships. Pepsi supplies drink syrup to its bottlers. The bottlers distribute to intermediate customers, but Pepsi's sales force builds collaborative relationships with key customers and bottlers, and the corporate marketing department directs marketing efforts to end-user consumers. Close, internal relationships are sustained between the marketing and sales organizations. Pepsi's US sales and profit performance has been impressive during the first decade of the twenty-first century. The soft drink producer's powerful market sensing capabilities are important contributors to its success.

Process structure – sales process alignment

Understanding and responding appropriately to the buying process of business customers provides a foundation for the creation of a 'best-practices' sales process by the sales organization (Page, 2006). This sales process aligns selling efforts directly to the specific buying situation of the customer and is an important element of the sales strategy. As discussed earlier, different sales processes are often used to interact with different strategic accounts and different customer segments. An effective sales process increases the likelihood of successful customer interactions. For example, a recent study found that coordinating the sales process with the timing of the customer's buying process increased sales and profits as well as improving the relationship quality between the customer and the firm (Kumar, Venkatesan, & Reinartz, 2008).

Implementing formal sales processes was one of the new factors in the World Class Sales Benchmark study (HR Chally, 2007) and is cited as one of the best practices of leading sales organizations (Page, 2006). The top sales organizations use formal sales processes as a basis for interacting with customers and for managing sales opportunities and salespeople. The effectiveness of these sales processes depends upon their alignment with the buying processes of customers. Proper alignment of the selling and buying processes improves the likelihood of the type of buyer/seller interaction that will result in co-creation of value.

Marketing–sales relationship alignment

The implementation of market and customer-oriented selling orientations increases the need for alignment between marketing and sales. One of the tenets of customer-oriented selling is that the sales organization (sales teams or individual salespeople) fulfill the role of strategic orchestrator within the firm (Corcoran, Petersen, Baitch, & Barrett, 1995). The salesperson or sales team coordinates all of the necessary people and knowledge that is necessary to meet customer requirements. Reporting relationships have little meaning under a true customer-oriented selling model, and cross-functional teams work together to serve the customer.

From a strategic perspective, two types of marketing and sales alignment are critical. First, marketing often provides materials used by salespeople in the sales process with specific customers. However, the marketing function typically focuses on developing materials to achieve a desired positioning within markets and market segments. Although these materials serve an important purpose, salespeople need materials that are directed at the particular needs of individual customers. The marketing and sales function need to work together to generate sales-support materials that salespeople can adapt to focus on the specific needs of individual customers.

Second, the use of multiple sales channels also requires alignment between marketing and sales. Marketing efforts, such as advertising and direct mail, are often used to generate leads and sometimes to qualify and prioritize prospects. The leads or prospects are then turned over to the sales organization for follow-up. Oftentimes, the leads or prospects generated from marketing efforts are viewed as poor opportunities by salespeople. The net result is that salespeople do not contact the leads or prospects and the firm loses potential sales opportunities. There needs to be close collaboration between sales and marketing to define a prospect profile and create marketing offers that produce desired opportunities for salespeople.

Firm metrics–sales organization strategy metrics alignment

Metrics used by the sales organization need to be aligned with the changes in metrics adopted by the firm and marketing function. The typical use of sales-related metrics is still important, but needs to be supplemented by metrics that focus more on profitability, such as account profitability, and long-term customer development, such as customer lifetime value and customer equity. These types of metrics are consistent with the market and customer-oriented selling orientations and with strategic relationships and sales strategies. Different metrics are likely needed for each strategic account and for different customer segments in the firm's sales strategy.

DHL's Asia-Pacific division, with a total of 1500 salespeople in 41 countries, redefined its metrics as part of a sales improvement process by identifying key revenue drivers, benchmarking, defining key improvement areas, measuring individual performance, and coaching first-line sales managers and salespeople (Rees & Diamond, 2008). Metrics were developed for new customer acquisition, customer development, customer retention, and salesforce efficiency and effectiveness. Although revamping metrics was a huge undertaking at DHL in the Asia-Pacific region, results have been impressive with an annual average 15% growth rate in recent years. Further, the inclusion of customer retention and customer development as key metrics will contribute to increasing customer value over time.

The linkages of market orientation–customer-oriented selling, strategic relationships–sales strategy, process structure–sales process, marketing–sales relationships, and firm metrics–sales organization metrics aligned to customer priorities provides the strategic foundation for a sales organization transformation. The final ingredient is to align sales management practice to provide the sales capabilities to support the sales organization strategy.

Sales management practice alignment

Sales management practice must be aligned with the strategic priorities of the sales organization to deliver superior customer value. Although the logic of this statement is fairly simple, it cannot be assumed that the necessary alignment will be achieved without dedicated efforts up, down, and across the sales organization (Matthyssens & Vandenbempt, 2008). We discuss how sales leaders and managers can play a key role in the alignment of sales management practices with sales organization strategy.

Customer-oriented selling–sales management alignment

Sales managers can take deliberate actions to establish a customer-oriented selling orientation by creating a customer-centric culture and climate, developing a customer-focused salesforce through recruiting, selecting, and training of salespeople, and directing the efforts of salespeople to follow the prescribed strategy.

The importance of organizational culture and organizational climate in supporting a customer-oriented selling strategy has been pointed out by sales researchers (Ingram et al., 2002; Martin & Bush, 2003; Schwepker, 2003). Organizational climate refers to employee perceptions about workplace norms and expectations as expressed in policies and procedures, and how those norms and expectations are reinforced through rewards and sanctions (Schneider & Rentsch, 1988). Organizational culture refers to shared assumptions and knowledge about how organizations function (Deshpandé & Webster, 1989).

To foster a customer-centric climate and culture, sales managers can emphasize recognition and support for salespeople's efforts, grant salespeople an appropriate level of job autonomy when dealing with customers, and encourage salespeople to be creative and innovative when meeting customer needs (Ingram et al., 2002; Martin & Bush, 2003). Further, to establish a customer-oriented sales organization climate and culture, Schwepker (2003) points out the importance of having a strong positive ethical climate which can be directly impacted by sales leaders and managers.

In recruiting salespeople and providing initial sales training, the concept of salesforce socialization can provide a guide to managerial action. Through the socialization process, salespeople assimilate the knowledge, skills, and values that are necessary for acceptable job performance (Dubinsky, Howell, Ingram, & Bellenger, 1986). One aspect of the socialization model proposed by Dubinsky et al. (1986) is congruence, which involves the matching of the capabilities of sales recruits with the needs of the sales organization. Assuming that an organization wishes to increase its use of customer-oriented selling, previous research indicates that salespeople's moral values and ability to build customer trust would be important job qualifications (Schwepker, 2003). These salesperson attributes are imbedded in a leading trust-building model which posits that salespeople build customer trust through interactions that demonstrate candor and a customer orientation (Swan, Bowers, & Richardson, 1999).

Moving past the recruiting and selection phase, role definition is an important step in the socialization process. Role definition prescribes the tasks to be performed and the priorities assigned to those tasks. Looking to the literature on customer-oriented selling gives some insights into how customer-oriented selling roles can be defined. First, it is important to convey and reinforce desired role behaviors by utilizing a behavior-based control system to monitor, direct, evaluate, and reward salespeople (Anderson & Oliver, 1987). This proposition is reinforced in studies of salespeople that found positive associations between the salespeople's customer-orientation and the elements of a behavior-based control system (Baldauf, Cravens, & Piercy, 2001a, 2001b; Cravens, Ingram, LaForge, & Young, 1993; O'Hara, Boles, & Johnston, 1991).

In keeping with premises of a behavior-based control system, sales researchers have suggested that the use of customer-oriented selling can be facilitated when sales managers build relationships with salespeople that are based on mutual trust, support, frequent interactions, and a mix of formal and informal rewards (Ingram, LaForge, Locander, Mackenzie, & Podsakoff, 2005; Schwepker, 2003). Further, Boles, Babin, Brashear, and Brooks (2001) found that customer-oriented selling is negatively linked to centralized decision making and positively linked to the firm's customer orientation. This reinforces the view of Martin and Bush (2003), who propose that the empowerment of salespeople is fundamental to achieving customer-oriented selling.

Sales strategy–sales management alignment

Sales management practice must be aligned with the sales strategies developed for strategic accounts and customer segments. The purpose of a sales strategy is to make it easy for customers to buy, but to also serve customers in a cost-effective manner. Of particular importance is designing a sales organization structure as a vehicle for implementing sales strategies. The basic alternatives are framed by questions such as:

- Should the salesforce be specialized? If specialization is needed, what is the basis for specialization – product, customer type, or industry?
- Should the firm have different salesforces that focus on different phases of the sales process (e.g. prospecting, sales support, winning customers, maintaining customers)?

- Should the firm use an employee (direct) salesforce or an indirect salesforce (e.g. manufacturers' representatives)?
- Should the selling function be outsourced entirely?

All too often, these decisions are based on what structure is already in place or on short-term economics. To build a structure that can endure marketplace dynamics, sales managers should develop the best structure to implement sales strategies successfully. Considerable attention needs to address the best structure for meeting the specific needs of strategic accounts.

A timeless example of the importance of this decision was Procter & Gamble's decision to move an account management team to Bentonville, Arkansas in the mid-1980s to serve Wal-Mart. P & G had been accustomed to calling the shots with its large retail customers. With a huge advertising and sales promotion budget pulling products through the channel, retail customers had little choice but to cooperate on P & G's terms. The P & G move to Bentonville was such a major development that it received front-page coverage in the *Wall Street Journal*. Many industry observers saw it as the end of the reign for P & G and a signal P & G had lost a power struggle with Wal-Mart. Twenty years later, with its status as a leading vendor to the world's largest retailer, P & G's decision to sell like Wal-Mart wanted to buy looks like a sound decision.

There is a clear trend toward the move to market-specialized sales organization structures. This is because the market-specialized approach aligns well with customer-focused selling and can be adapted to different sales strategies. An example of this approach is National Oilwell Varco (NOV), a global manufacturer, distributor, and service provider of equipment for offshore oil and gas drilling rigs (James, 2008). NOV transitioned from a product-based sales organization structure to a customer-focused structure which assigned newly appointed global account managers to coordinate sales activity across three NOV business units for their largest customers such as ExxonMobil. This allowed NOV to facilitate purchasing within its global accounts and provide the total solution of products and services desired by the larger accounts.

As discussed earlier, customer prioritization and segmentation, and sales channel decisions, are an important part of the development of sales strategy. Progressive sales organizations are becoming more analytical in weighing the alternatives in these areas. For example, a large global banking and financial services firm worked with sales consultant ZS Associates to move away from a telephone-based sales effort by 12 sales representatives who actively worked with approximately 2500 mutual fund wholesalers across the USA (Canady, 2008). The company decided to reduce the number of wholesalers it worked with and to feature an in-person call coverage strategy with 40 sales representatives to work with a smaller number of more influential wholesalers. An important input into the analysis preceding this highly successful change was analytical software used by ZS Associates to map territories to approximately equalize opportunities within territories without disrupting existing salesperson–customer relationships.

Sales process–sales management alignment

Sales managers need to focus on developing specific sales processes for strategic accounts and customer segments, and then use these processes as a basis for sales management activities. Involving field sales managers in sales process development has been found to be an effective way to give these managers ownership of the process. This increases the likelihood that the field sales managers will use the sales processes as a basis for sales training and coaching efforts (Page, 2006). The alignment of sales processes and sales management activities is critical for the co-creation of value by salespeople with customers.

The sales process has typically been described as five to seven steps to include prospecting, pre-call planning, sales presentation delivery, overcoming resistance, and closing the sale. In recent years, post-sale follow-up has been added to some versions of the sales process and the term closing the sale is more frequently referred to as earning buyer commitment. These changes to the traditional sales process signal that buyer–seller interactions are changing to reflect greater involvement of the buyer in the process, and that the buyer has gained relative power in buyer–seller interactions. As noted by Sheth and Sharma (2008), the time has come to reconsider traditional depictions of the sales process.

Sales processes vary significantly according to how much the seller adapts to different selling situations and how much they adapt to buyer reactions during specific sales encounters. Sales processes also vary extensively according to how much the salesperson focuses on buyer's unique needs and strategic priorities. Sales processes that are low in the level of adaptive selling and do not focus strongly on the buyer's unique needs and/or strategic priorities are not typically customer oriented (Ingram et al., 2009). These processes include the stimulus-response model, or canned sales pitches as typified by telemarketing sales calls. Another popular, though not particularly customer-oriented sales process model, is the A-I-D-A (Attention, Interest, Desire, Action) approach which attempts to move customers through the mental states leading to a purchase.

Among the more customer-oriented sales models are problem-solving, needs satisfaction, and consultative selling. In terms of re-thinking the sales process, we advocate the use of these three sales models to fit the situation. Consultative selling is appropriate when the customer is willing to share strategic priorities with the seller and sees the seller as being capable of supporting the customer's strategic initiatives. Otherwise, problem solution or needs satisfaction models can be implemented as genuine customer-oriented sales processes.

Consultative, problem solution, and needs satisfaction selling involve a two-way discourse with the customer, far more conversational than is achieved with other sales models which rely more on presenting than listening to the customer. The business conversations that are an integral part of customer-oriented selling are ultimately driven by an overarching purpose – to enhance customer value. With this purpose in place, a sales process that aligns with the mandate to build superior customer value could be defined by these elements (Ingram et al., 2009):

- Assess the prospective customer's situation and buying processes.
- Discover the prospective customer's specific needs and requirements, and how the customer defines value.
- Confirm the prospective customer's strategic priorities.
- Illustrate how the sales organization can create and deliver customer value.
- Negotiate an agreement to do business.
- Assess the extent to which the customer is satisfied with the value received.
- Build increasing levels of customer value by providing additional opportunities over an extended time horizon.

Another concrete way in which sales managers can align with a customer-oriented sales strategy is to integrate service recovery into the sales process (Gonzalez, Hoffman, & Ingram, 2005). Given the inevitability of at least occasional service failures, and the role of the salesperson in the continual delivery of increasing levels of customer value, future conceptualizations of the sales process should address how salespeople can build lasting customer relationships through a service dimension. This view is consistent with the service-dominant logic, which holds that a service-centered view is customer-oriented and relational (Vargo & Lusch, 2004). Support for the integration of sales and service roles is also found in the work of Ulaga and Eggert (2006), who found that service support and personal interaction are core differentiators in business relationships.

Marketing and sales relationship–sales management alignment

Exploring the origins of the conflicts between sales and marketing is beyond the scope of this paper, but existing research indicates that the interactions between marketing and sales are complex, and that relationships between the two areas are often problematic (Homburg & Jensen, 2007; Le Meunier-Fitzhugh & Piercy, 2007). Given the historical lack of coordination between marketing and sales and the current and future importance of maximizing customer value, sales leaders and managers must play a more active role in aligning the sales and marketing functions. We propose that given the dynamics and difficulties inherent in most marketplaces, it is incumbent upon the sales organization to enhance collaboration and alignment with marketing by taking an outreach-oriented approach to foster more cooperative efforts between sales and marketing.

In aligning sales management activities and practice to enhance productive efforts between sales and marketing, it is also important for sales leaders to consider their own attitudes and behaviors, along with the established sales culture in the firm. Whether fair or not, there is often a perception that sales personnel operate with an independence that is fiercely protected by the sales organization. The old saying that 'sales produces the revenue, all other departments are just overhead' may have been intended to build pride in the sales organizations, but the oversimplification in the statement can certainly contribute to friction with marketing and other functional areas. More specifically, the sales organization's pride of customer ownership and resulting lack of willingness to share information has contributed heavily to numerous failed customer relationship management initiatives. Sales managers should become catalytic agents, advocating that the entire firm embraces the concept of the learning organization, particularly as it relates to market sensing and understanding customers. This effort should be supported by the initiation of cross-training on collaboration, joint goal-setting, and common rewards (Kahn, Reizenstein, & Rentz, 2004).

Sales organization strategy metrics–sales management alignment

There is little question that traditional sales metrics and corresponding reward systems have been detrimental to fostering customer-oriented selling and long-term customer relationships (Ingram, 1996). The use of the compensation system as an automatic supervisory aid is especially problematic when straight commission compensation systems are used to drive total sales revenue without regard for alternative metrics such as customer satisfaction and retention.

Investment sales personnel such as stock brokers and mortgage loan officers have based their sales behaviors on the wrong metrics for decades. Now these industries have lost a large measure of customer trust and customer equity due to misplaced metrics. The US pharmaceutical industry, which has persisted in a non-customer-oriented sales process that trades on the personal aspect of customer relationships, now finds that regulatory bodies and the medical community are dictating changes to long-standing sales practices.

Given these examples, it seems prudent for sales organizations to align their metrics and reward systems with the overall goal of maximizing customer value.

For many firms, the reconsideration of appropriate metrics and how to align these metrics with an emphasis on customer value will require the sales organization to become less tactical, and more strategic. Instead of focusing strictly on sales volume, salespeople will become more concerned with managing customers as assets. Profitability will increasingly become an important metric, as will share of customer, customer loyalty, and customer retention.

To select the proper metrics and encourage efforts toward those metrics, it will be important for sales managers to gain a deeper understanding of the drivers of sales productivity, including how individual salespeople's behavior impacts desired outcomes. A comprehensive review of the sales management control systems literature concludes: 'Research findings point to a positive influence of behavior control on sales organization effectiveness (e.g., sales, market share, profitability, and customer satisfaction), as well as other overall performance measures' (Baldauf, Cravens, & Piercy, 2005, p. 24).

Sales organization implications and research directions

We have discussed the importance of strategic alignment to the success of firm and sales organization transformations and highlighted key alignment linkages between sales organization strategy and firm transformation strategy and between sales management practice and sales organization strategy. All of these efforts must be aligned to create and deliver superior value to customers. Our discussion has important implications for sales organizations and suggests key areas for future research.

The critical implication for sales organizations is the need to consider the key alignment linkages we have presented. Sales organization strategy and sales management practice decisions are not made in isolation. Decisions in each area are interrelated to other areas and these interrelationships need to be proactively examined as part of the decision-making process. This is especially true during firm strategic transformation efforts which require proper alignment with a sales organization transformation to be successful. The linkages in Table 1 provide a framework for sales organizations to guide decisions that will result in proper alignment among critical areas.

There are many opportunities for research in this area. One basic need is to define the alignment construct more rigorously. The term alignment is used often by practitioners and researchers, but the domain and dimensionality of the construct has received limited attention. Therefore, the term is used to mean different things by different people. A more rigorous and accepted definition of alignment would set the stage for future research efforts.

Another stream of research should identify the key alignment areas and specific linkages required for firm and sales organization transformation. We have presented five basic areas and suggested specific linkages at the firm, sales organization strategy, and sales management practice levels for each area. There may be other areas that need to be included and other linkages of importance among these areas. In fact, many of the linkages we suggest have received only limited research attention. The competitive and turbulent business environment is likely to force firms to engage in more strategic transformations in the future. Sales organization transformations will play an increasingly important role in the success of these firm transformations. Therefore, more attention to specific linkages requiring alignment is needed by sales organizations and sales researchers.

References

Ambler, T., & Roberts, J. (2006). *Beware the silver metric: Marketing performance measurement has to be multidimensional* (Marketing Science Institute Report 06-003). Cambridge, MA: Marketing Science Institute.

Anderson, E., & Oliver, R.L. (1987). Perspectives on behavior-based versus outcome-based salesforce control systems. *Journal of Marketing, 51*(October), 76–88.

Baldauf, A., Cravens, D.W., & Piercy, N.F. (2001a). Examining business strategy, sales management, and salesperson antecedents of sales organization effectiveness. *Journal of Personal Selling & Sales Management, 21*(2), 109–122.

Baldauf, A., Cravens, D.W., & Piercy, N.F. (2001b). Examining the consequences of sales management control strategies in European field sales organizations. *International Marketing Review, 18*(5), 474–508.

Baldauf, A., Cravens, D.W., & Piercy, N.F. (2005). Sales management control research: Synthesis and an agenda for future research. *Journal of Personal Selling & Sales Management, 25*(1), 7–26.

Boles, J.S., Babin, B.J., Brashear, T.G., & Brooks, C. (2001). An examination of the relationships between retail work environments, salesperson selling orientation–customer orientation and job performance. *Journal of Marketing Theory Practice, 9*(Summer), 1–13.

Canady, H. (2008). A high-value sales channel. *Selling Power, 28*(6), 103–104.

Cespedes, F.V. (1995). *Concurrent marketing*. Boston, MA: Harvard Business School Press.

Clark, B.H. (2001). A summary of thinking on measuring the value of marketing. *Journal of Targeting, Measurement and Analysis for Marketing, 9*(4), 357–369.

Corcoran, K.J., Petersen, L.K., Baitch, D.B., & Barrett, M.F. (1995). *High performing sales organizations*. Chicago, IL: Irwin Professional Publishing.

Cravens, D.W. (2006). Strategic marketing's global challenges and opportunities. *Handbook of Business Strategy, 7*(1), 63–70.

Cravens, D.W., & Piercy, N.F. (2009). *Strategic marketing* (9th ed.). Burr Ridge, IL: McGraw-Hill Irwin.

Cravens, D.W., Ingram, T.N., LaForge, R.W., & Young, C.E. (1993). Behavior-based and outcome-based salesforce control systems. *Journal of Marketing, 57*(October), 47–59.

Cravens, D.W., Piercy, N.F., & Low, G.S. (2006). Globalization of the sales organization: Management control and its consequences. *Organizational Dynamics, 35*(3), 291–303.

Cross, M., Brashear, T.G., Rigdon, E.E., & Bellenger, D.N. (2007). Customer orientation and salesperson performance. *European Journal of Marketing, 41*(7/8), 821–835.

Day, G.S. (1990). *Market-driven strategy: Processes for creating value*. New York: Free Press.

Day, G.S. (1994). The capabilities of market-driven organizations. *Journal of Marketing, 58*(October), 37–52.

Day, G.S. (1997). Aligning the organization to the market. In D.R. Lehman & K.E. Jocz (Eds.), *Reflections on the futures of marketing* (p. 72). Cambridge, MA: Marketing Science Institute.

Day, G.S. (2005). *Aligning the organization with the market* (Marketing Science Institute Report 05-110). Cambridge, MA: Marketing Science Institute.

Deshpandé, R., & Farley, J.V. (2004). Organizational culture, market orientation, innovativeness, and firm performance: An international research odyssey. *International Journal of Research in Marketing, 21*(1), 3–22.

Desphande, R., & Webster, Jr., F.E. (1989). Organizational culture and marketing: Defining the research agenda. *Journal of Marketing, 53*(1), 3–15.

Dubinsky, A.J., Howell, R.D., Ingram, T.N., & Bellenger, D.N. (1986). Salesforce socialization. *Journal of Marketing, 50*(October), 192–207.

Economist, The. (2005, April 9). The cart pulling the horse. *The Economist*, p. 5.

Ernst, D., & Bamford, J. (2005). Your alliances are too stable. *Harvard Business Review, 83*(6), 133–141.

Ferris, P.W., Bendle, N.T., Pfeifer, P.E., & Reibstein, D. (2006). *Marketing metrics: 50+ metrics every executive should master*. Upper Saddle River, NJ: Wharton School Publishing/Pearson Education.

Franke, G.R., & Park., J. (2006). Salesperson adaptive selling behavior and customer orientation: A meta-analysis. *Journal of Marketing Research, 43*(4), 693–702.

Gonzalez, G.R., Hoffman, K.D., & Ingram, T.N. (2005). Improving relationship selling through failure analysis and recovery efforts: A framework and call to action. *Journal of Personal Selling & Sales Management*, 25(1), 57–65.

Guenzi, P., & Troilo, G. (2007). The joint contribution of marketing and sales to the creation of superior customer value. *Journal of Business Research*, 60(2), 98–107.

Homburg, C., Droll, M., & Totzek, D. (2008). Customer prioritization: does it pay off, and how should it be implemented? *Journal of Marketing*, 72(5), 110–130.

Homburg, C., & Jensen, O. (2007). The thought worlds of marketing and sales: Which differences make a difference? *Journal of Marketing*, 71(July), 124–142.

Homburg, C., Jensen, O., & Krohmer, H. (2008). Configurations of marketing and sales: A taxonomy. *Journal of Marketing*, 72(March), 133–154.

HR Chally (2007). *The Chally world class sales excellence research report*. Dayton, Ohio: The HR Chally Group.

Humphreys, M., & Williams, M.R. (1996). Exploring the relative effects of salesperson interpersonal process attributes and technical product attributes on customer satisfaction. *Journal of Personal Selling & Sales Management*, 16(3), 47–57.

Hunter, G.K., & Perreault, W.D., Jr. (2007). Making sales technology effective. *Journal of Marketing*, 71(January), 16–34.

Ingram, T.N. (1996). Relationship selling: Moving from rhetoric to reality. *Mid-American Journal of Business*, 11(1), 5–12.

Ingram, T.N., LaForge, R.W., Avila, R.A., Schwepker, C.H., Jr, & Williams, M.R. (2009). *Sales management: Analysis and decision making*. Armonk, NY: M.E. Sharpe.

Ingram, T.N., LaForge, R.W., & Leigh, T.W. (2002). Selling in the new millennium: A joint agenda. *Industrial Marketing Management*, 31(7), 559–567.

Ingram, T.N., LaForge, R.W., Locander, W.B., MacKenzie, S.B., & Podsakoff, P.M. (2005). New directions in sales leadership research. *Journal of Personal Selling & Sales Management*, 25(2), 137–154.

James, G. (2008). Keep the focus on strategic accounts. *Selling Power*, 28(5), 17–20.

Kahn, K.B., Reizenstein, R.C., & Rentz, J.O. (2004). Sales-distribution interfunctional climate and relationship effectiveness. *Journal of Business Research*, 57(October), 1085–1091.

Kirca, A.H., Jayachandran, S., & Bearden, W.O. (2005). Market orientation: A meta-analytic review and assessment of its antecedents and impact on performance. *Journal of Marketing*, 69(April), 24–41.

Kocabasoglu, C., & Suresh, N.C. (2006). Strategic sourcing: An empirical investigation of the concept and its practices in U.S. manufacturing firms. *The Journal of Supply Chain Management*, 42(2), 4–16.

Kotler, P., Rackham, N., & Krishnaswamy, S. (2006). Ending the war between sales and marketing. *Harvard Business Review*, 84(7–8), 68–78.

Kumar, V., Venkatesan, R., & Reinartz, W. (2008). Performance implication of adopting a customer-focused sales campaign. *Journal of Marketing*, 72(5), 50–68.

Lehmann, D.R. (2004). Metrics for making marketing matter. *Journal of Marketing*, 68(4), 73–75.

Le Meunier-Fitzhugh, K., & Piercy, N.F. (2007). Does collaboration between sales and marketing affect business performance? *Journal of Personal Selling and Sales Management*, 27(3), 207–220.

Martin, C.A., & Bush, A.J. (2003). The potential influence of organizational and personal variables on customer-oriented selling. *Journal of Business and Industrial Marketing*, 18(2), 114–132.

Matthyssens, P., & Vandenbempt, K. (2008). Moving from basic offerings to value-added solutions: Strategies, barriers and alignment. *Industrial Marketing Management*, 37, 316–328.

O'Hara, B.S., Boles, J.S., & Johnston, M.W. (1991). The influence of personal variables on salesperson selling orientation. *Journal of Personal Selling & Sales Management*, 11(1), 61–67.

O'Sullivan, D., & Abela, A.V. (2007). Marketing performance measurement ability and firm performance. *Journal of Marketing*, 72(2), 79–93.

Page, R. (2006). *Make winning a habit*. New York: McGraw-Hill.

Piercy, N.F., & Lane, N. (2005). Strategic imperatives for transformation of the sales organization. *Journal of Change Management*, 5(3), 249–266.

Rees, M., & Diamond, S. (2008). Textbook case study. *Selling Power*, 28(6), 29, 35.

Roberts, J. (2004). *The modern firm*. London: Oxford University Press.

Saxe, R., & Weitz, B.A. (1982). The SOCO scale: A measure of the customer orientation of salespeople. *Journal of Marketing Research*, *19*(August), 343–351.

Schneider, B., & Rentsch, J. (1988). Managing climates and cultures: A futures perspective. In J. Hage (Ed.), *Futures of organizations* (pp. 181–200). Lexington, MA: Lexington Books.

Schultz, R.J., & Good, D.J. (2000). Impact of the consideration of future sales consequences and customer-oriented selling on long-term buyer–seller relationships. *Journal of Business & Industrial Marketing*, *15*(4), 200–215.

Schwepker, C.H. Jr. (2003). Customer-oriented selling: A review, extension and directions for future research. *Journal of Personal Selling & Sales Management*, *23*(2), 151–171.

Sheth, J.N., & Sharma, S. (2008). The impact of the product to service shift in industrial markets and the evolution of the sales organization. *Industrial Marketing Management*, *37*(3), 260–269.

Slater, S.F., & Narver, J.C. (1994). Market orientation, customer value, and superior performance. *Business Horizons*, *37*(2), 22–27.

Stevens, H., & Kinni, T. (2007). *Achieve sales excellence*. Avon, MA: Platinum Press.

Swan, J.E., Bowers, M.R., & Richardson, L.D. (1999). Customer trust in the salesperson: An integrative review and meta-analysis of the empirical literature. *Journal of Business Research*, *44*(February), 93–107.

Tam, P. (2006, April 3). Hurd's big challenge at H-P: Overhauling corporate sales. *Wall Street Journal*, pp. A1, A13.

Ulaga, W., & Eggert, A. (2006). Value-based differentiation in business relationships: Gaining and sustaining key supplier status. *Journal of Marketing*, *70*(1), 119–136.

Vargo, S.L., & Lusch, R.F. (2004). Evolving to a new dominant logic for marketing. *Journal of Marketing*, *68*(1), 1–23.

Verhoef, P.C., & Leeflang, P.S.H. (2008). *Getting marketing back in the boardroom: Understanding the drivers of marketing's influence within the firm* (Marketing Science Institute Report No. 08-104, pp. 83–114). Cambridge, MA: Marketing Science Institute.

Webster, F.E., Jr. (1997). The future role of marketing in the organization. In D.R. Lehmann & K.E. Jocz (Eds.), *Reflections on the future of marketing* (pp. 39–66). Cambridge, MA: Marketing Science Institute.

Wilding, R. (2006, November 10). Playing to the tune of shared success. *Financial Times Report: Understanding Collaboration*, pp. 2–3.

Workman, J.P., Homburg, C., & Gruner, K. (1998). Marketing organization: An integrative framework of dimensions and determinants. *Journal of Marketing*, *62*(July), 21–41.

Developing a strategic framework of key account performance

Eli Jones, Keith A. Richards, Diane Halstead and Frank Q. Fu

Strategic management of key accounts has become an important component of many companies' sales efforts. This research introduces a strategic framework of key account performance that integrates theory from relationship marketing, key account management, and customer equity. Using the three drivers of customer equity – value equity, brand equity, and relationship equity – the framework captures both the relational outcomes (relationship commitment and trust) and financial performance outcomes (profitability and share of spend) of strategic decisions made in key account programs. Implications and future research are then discussed.

Introduction

Major shifts are taking place in the sales management landscape. Changes in technology, greater numbers of demanding customers, hypercompetitive markets, and calls for higher legal and ethical standards are forcing companies to reshape their sales efforts at an unprecedented rate (Jones, Brown, Zoltners, & Weitz, 2005). In the wake of these changes, selling companies have sought greater levels of partnership and commitment with their largest, most important accounts (Piercy & Lane, 2003). The movement toward these larger accounts and a desire for stronger relationships has spawned great interest in strategic account management (Leigh & Marshall, 2001). Accordingly, key account management has become an important strategic tool in securing and keeping a selling company's best customers.

Key accounts are defined as customers in business-to-business markets identified by the selling company as their most important customers and serviced by the selling company with dedicated resources (Workman, Homburg, & Jensen, 2003). Much of the research on these important accounts has focused on key account performance (e.g. Ryals, 2006; Sengupta, Krapfel, & Pusateri, 2000; Workman et al., 2003). Key account performance has been conceptualized as both relationship quality/effectiveness (Sengupta et al., 2000) and as an objective measure such as market performance or profitability (Homburg, Workman, & Jensen, 2002; Ryals & Holt, 2007). Several studies suggest that the relational outcomes lead to financial performance (e.g. Workman et al., 2003). Regardless of the measure, however, explaining and predicting key account performance has been a central goal since key account research began to emerge within the sales literature (see Homburg et al., 2002 for a review).

Despite this emphasis on account performance, however, little research has been directed toward developing a strategic framework for understanding key account performance. That is, the links between various key account program strategies and their resulting impact on key account performance have not yet been integrated into a comprehensive model. Yet as companies shift toward becoming more customer-centric, key account managers must be more strategic and have 'more of a business and financial perspective than that used by traditional sales representatives' (Homburg, Workman, & Jensen, 2000, p. 475). In fact, key account managers must have skill sets 'more similar to those of general managers' (Homburg et al., 2000, p. 476). Account managers are responsible for not only selling to and servicing their best customers, but also for developing strategies to capture financial value (Ryals & Rogers, 2007). Thus, any new model of key account performance should consider the impact of strategic decisions made in the key account program, and it must consider their impact on both the quality of the relationship and the level of financial performance.

The goal of this research, therefore, is to propose a conceptual model of key account performance that links strategic marketing decisions in the key account program (e.g. increasing promotion/merchandising support to enhance brand equity) with important marketing outcomes (e.g. increases in relationship trust and profitability). Drawing on academic research in the areas of relationship marketing, key account management, and customer equity, a strategic framework for key account performance is developed. Customer equity is employed because it integrates a strategic decision-making approach that is customer-centered, theoretical, and practical enough for managerial application (Rust, Lemon, & Zeithaml, 2004). The framework begins with the three building blocks of customer equity: value equity, brand equity, and relationship equity (Rust, Zeithaml, & Lemon, 2000). The equity variables are then related to two relational mediators, trust and commitment, which are incorporated from traditional key account models (e.g. Sengupta et al., 2000; Workman et al., 2003) and are considered essential to successful business partnerships (Morgan & Hunt, 1994). Commitment and trust are then evaluated in terms of their impact on account performance (as measured by profitability and share of spend) in order to create a strategic framework of key account performance.

Toward that end, a review of the research on key accounts and relationship marketing is provided, followed by a brief summary of the customer equity literature. The conceptual model of key account performance is then introduced, and research propositions based on the strategic framework are offered. Finally, implications for managers and researchers are presented.

Theoretical background

Key account research

Much of the key account (KA) research can be classified broadly into studies of KA management at either the organizational level or at the personal level. At the organizational level, some studies investigated the appropriateness of KA programs (Sengupta, Krapfel, & Pusateri, 1997a, 1997b; Shapiro & Moriarty, 1980, 1984), while others examined how selling companies should organize to support KA programs (Dishman & Nitse, 1998; Homburg et al., 2002; Montgomery & Yip, 2000; Workman et al., 2003). Some of the organizational studies looked at KA activities such as pricing and logistics, which could be viewed somewhat as strategic in nature (e.g. Workman et al.,

2003), but rather than focusing on the activity or strategy itself, their research looked at the *intensity* and *proactiveness* of the activities.

The second classification of KA research explored primarily the types of individuals or teams who are best suited to manage KAs (Boles, Barksdale, & Johnson, 1996; Sengupta et al., 2000; Wotruba & Castleberry, 1993). These studies typically looked at personal characteristics, team traits, and/or relationship building skills (e.g. Sengupta et al., 2000). This research found, for example, that the most effective KA managers have intrapreneurial abilities (Sengupta et al., 2000), are innovative (Wotruba & Castleberry, 1993), and sometimes take risks in order to serve their KAs (Kuratko, Montagno, & Hornsby, 1990). In addition, KA team members form better relationships with their KA counterparts when there is a certain 'esprit de corps' in the supplier organization (Workman et al., 2003).

Studies at both the organizational level and the personal level examined KA performance where it has been defined as both a relational variable (Sengupta et al., 2000) and as a financial performance variable (e.g. market share or profitability, Homburg et al., 2002; Ryals & Holt, 2007). Some research found that relational outcomes can impact financial outcomes (Workman et al., 2003). For example, profitability was used as a measure of KA performance by Homburg et al. (2002) as one of the outcomes of KA relationship effectiveness. Profitability was also the focus of the KA performance research conducted by Ryals (2006) and Ryals and Holt (2007), although their primary emphasis on profitability was on measures of customer lifetime value. Vogel, Evanschitzky, and Ramaseshan (2008, p. 98), however, argue that customer lifetime value is simply too difficult for most companies to measure, and that, while a worthwhile ambition, measuring it 'remains a pipe dream for most companies'.

Despite the previous studies in both classifications of KA research, there is still a need to investigate KA program strategy and its impact on relationship and performance variables. Although these two categories of KA research differ in level of analysis, they often share a common theoretical structure based on relationship marketing models (e.g. Morgan & Hunt, 1994). This aspect of KA research is addressed next.

KA research and relationship marketing

Much of the KA research has centered on models of relationship marketing (Morgan & Hunt, 1994; Smith & Barclay, 1997). Many of these models have the following form: antecedents, at either the organizational level or the KA manager level, are tied to relational mediators (e.g. trust, communication quality, relationship commitment, conflict reduction) which ultimately lead to some level of KA performance (e.g. Homburg et al., 2002; Ryals, 2006; Schultz & Evans, 2002; Sengupta et al., 2000; Workman et al., 2003).

The Morgan and Hunt (1994) commitment–trust theory of relationship marketing explores the nature of relationship marketing and proposes that commitment and trust should serve as two key mediating variables between relationship antecedents (e.g. relationship termination costs, shared values, communication) and different outcomes (e.g. acquiescence, cooperation, functional conflict). This structure places commitment and trust at the heart of the relational model. Palmatier, Dant, and Grewal (2007) compared four common theoretical perspectives of interorganizational relationship performance and found evidence that commitment and trust remain important mediators and direct antecedents to relationship performance measures, further supporting their place in these frameworks.

The first of these two key mediating variables, relationship commitment, is defined as 'an exchange partner believing that an ongoing relationship with another is so important as to warrant maximum efforts at maintaining it; that is, the committed party believes the relationship is worth working to ensure that it endures indefinitely' (Morgan & Hunt, 1994, p. 23). KA relationships are built on the idea of commitment, and relationship importance is part of what defines a KA. KA customers agree to forgo other suppliers (not all, perhaps, but many other suppliers) allowing KA suppliers to centralize management teams, dedicate special resources, increase their activities, and above all else, attach incredible importance to their KAs (Homburg et al., 2000; Montgomery & Yip, 2000). Commitment is an essential component of effective long-term relationships (Gundlach, Achrol, & Mentzer, 1995; Morgan & Hunt, 1994).

Trust is the second key mediating variable in the commitment–trust theory and is considered to be central to successful partnerships. It is defined as the confidence that one relational partner has in the other's reliability and integrity (Morgan & Hunt, 1994, p. 24) and implies the behavioral intention of 'willingness to rely' on the other partner. Various determinants and consequences of trust have been explored in the context of buyer–seller relationships, channel relationships, and other marketing relationship contexts (e.g. Anderson & Narus, 1990; Dwyer, Schurr, & Oh, 1987; Moorman, Deshpande, & Zaltman, 1993). Long-term relationships such as those characterized by KAs and their suppliers generally have high levels of trust and commitment because both partners work on maintaining the relationship indefinitely in order to achieve mutual benefits (Morgan & Hunt, 1994). Trust and commitment are critical factors to business relationship success, and trust is often viewed as a major determinant of relationship commitment (Achrol, 1991; Moorman, Zaltman, & Deshpande, 1992; Morgan & Hunt, 1994).

Customer equity

Customer equity can be considered a gauge of the overall health of the organization in that it represents the 'total of the discounted lifetime values of all of its customers' (Rust et al., 2000, p. 4). As such, it constitutes not only the current profitability of customers, but future profits to be earned over some relevant time horizon. While the value of a firm's customer relationships does not represent the entire value of a firm (it excludes physical assets and intellectual property, for example), customer equity is an important strategic asset that should be carefully 'monitored and nurtured by firms to maximize long-term performance' (Vogel et al., 2008, p. 98). While the customer equity models have primarily been used to explain customer behavior in business-to-consumer environments (B2C), both Rust et al. (2000) and Ryals and Holt (2007) confirm that customer equity models should be useful in business-to-business (B2B) contexts as well. As would be expected, we assume a B2B context for our study of KAs.

A firm's source of customer equity is found in the drivers or building blocks of customer equity: value equity, brand equity, and relationship equity (Lemon, Rust, & Zeithaml, 2001; Rust et al., 2000, 2004). *Value equity* represents a customer's objective evaluation of a brand's utility based on an assessment of what is given up for what is received (Rust et al., 2000, p. 56). It is considered to be a rational, objective view of a firm's product or service offering and typically has been found to center around price, quality, and convenience (e.g. Rust et al., 2004; Vogel et al., 2008). Value equity is considered to be the core driver of customer equity in that, without a perception of some minimum value in the product/service, there is no basis upon which to form either relationship equity or brand equity.

Brand equity refers to the customer's subjective appraisal of the brand – a more intangible, emotional view that looks beyond any objective perception of the brand (Rust et al., 2004). Brand equity represents the value attached to a product or service that exists above and beyond the value of the physical product itself and its benefits (Keller, 2008). Brand equity captures elements of a brand (e.g. awareness and information) as well as corporate characteristics (e.g. corporate citizenship, ethical standards, and community events) (Rust et al., 2004). Brand equity increases when past marketing investments in the brand (e.g. advertising campaigns) add value to a brand by raising awareness and creating strong, unique, and favorable associations about the brand in consumers' minds (Keller, 2008).

Relationship equity encompasses the tendency of the customer to stay in a relationship with a brand/company and includes all the elements that link the buyer and seller together such as loyalty and affinity programs, community programs, and special reward and recognition programs (Rust et al., 2000; Rust, Lemon, & Zeithaml, 2001). Relationship equity captures the preferential treatment and special recognition provided to important customers as well as procedural knowledge that the customer acquires while in a relationship (Rust et al., 2004). Relationship equity goes beyond any objective or subjective evaluation of a brand or company. The focus is on the relationship between the customer and the selling organization and the customer's familiarity with and attraction to staying with the selling organization. Relationship equity for the buyer is built on common or shared experiences with the seller and may lead to a sense of pride in being party to the relationship.

Given the definitions of relationship commitment and relationship equity, further clarification is needed to ensure the conceptual distinctions between the two constructs. Relationship commitment, especially in a KA context, differs from relationship equity in several important ways. First, central to the concept of relationship commitment is the idea of *effort* – effort at unity (Dwyer et al., 1987), effort at preserving and advancing the relationship so as to maintain its value (Moorman et al., 1992; Morgan & Hunt, 1994), and joint efforts at planning and performance (Dwyer et al., 1987). Morgan and Hunt (1994, p. 23) argue that commitment occurs when a relationship is so important that it 'warrants maximum efforts' at maintaining it. Effort expended to reduce conflict, resolve conflict productively, avoid opportunism, or engage in other healthy relationship behaviors is not integral to the concept of relationship equity. In fact, there is evidence that some consumers, even while enjoying certain superficial benefits of 'relationship' marketing (e.g. price discounts with loyalty programs), avoid relationships with marketers for the very reason that it requires effort (Noble & Phillips, 2004).

A second difference between relationship equity and relationship commitment, opportunistic behavior, is probably fairly common in relationship equity programs (on the part of both the firm and customer), whereas forbearance of opportunism is more closely associated with trust and commitment (Morgan & Hunt, 1994; Smith & Barclay, 1997). Even disproportionate commitment in B2B relationships may not always lead to opportunistic behaviors (Gundlach et al., 1995).

Finally, Gundlach et al.'s (1995) concept of the *input* or *instrumental* component of commitment represents a third distinction between relationship commitment versus relationship equity. Equity does not include the concept of input – the idea of exchange partners taking affirmative actions that are actually 'difficult or impossible to redeploy to another exchange', actions that are 'analogous to exit barriers' even though they are voluntarily erected (Gundlach et al., 1995, p. 79). Loyalty programs such as those included in relationship equity typically employ no such structural ties or bonds. Thus, while clearly related, relationship equity and relationship commitment do not appear to represent the same underlying construct. The theoretical model proposed here assumes the three drivers of customer equity, value equity, brand equity, and relationship equity, will be directly impacted by the strategic decisions made in the KA program and in turn, impact either trust or commitment (or both).

Theoretical model and propositions

The proposed strategic framework of KA performance has a four-part structure: (1) strategic decisions made in the KA program, which result in (2) improvements in value equity, brand equity, and relationship equity, which lead to (3) greater relationship commitment and trust (relational mediators), which ultimately drive (4) KA performance (i.e. profitability and share of spend) (see Figure 1). Lemon et al. (2001, p. 21) suggest that customer equity puts the 'strategies that grow the value of customers at the heart of the organization'. To investigate the impact of the three types of equity in the proposed model, some examples of strategic decisions made in KA programs are first briefly summarized.

Strategic marketing decisions in KA programs

For a better understanding of the types of strategic decisions that KA managers make, Figure 2 is provided. Figure 2 shows common KA strategy decisions that require account managers to compete for marketing resources and that result in changes in KA customer perceptions, actions, and choices. These strategies are more explicit and comprehensive than Rust et al.'s (2004, p. 113) 'strategic investment categories'. The Figure is organized according to the traditional marketing mix or 'Four Ps' classification. In the product/service category, for example, it shows that a common KA strategy of tailoring a client's products to meet customized specifications is likely to increase value equity. Value equity is increased by increasing the buyer's perception of utility in terms of what is received versus what is given up. It could also increase utility by increasing the customer's perception of product quality, which would also lead to higher value equity.

In the promotion area, a cooperative advertising campaign between the supplier of a branded component part (e.g. Intel microchips) and a KA manufacturer (e.g. Dell computers) in which advertising costs are shared (because in the ads both the end product and the branded component are promoted) would likely increase brand equity as well as

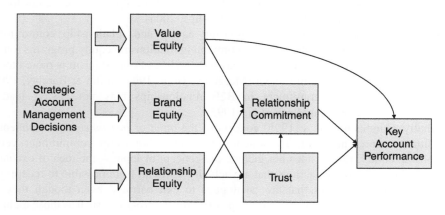

Figure 1.   Theoretical model.

Product/Service Strategies	Equity Increase	Pricing Strategies	Equity Increase
Customization of products or service offering to suit KA special needs	Value equity	Customized pricing deals and special offers due to KA status	Value equity
Free samples and new product trials before full market availability	Value equity	Sharing cost savings with KA as a result of reorganization, goal reformulation, outsourcing, or other strategic initiative	Value equity/ Relationship equity
Provision of informal consultancy services at no additional charge	Value equity		
Introduction of formal consulting services for KA for purchase	Value equity	Special credit/financing terms	Value equity
Provision of customized CRM data to assist client with various business plans	Value equity/ Relationship equity	Product replacements, in any condition, at no charge, no questions asked	Value equity/ Relationship equity
Distribution Strategies	**Equity Increase**	**Promotion Strategies**	**Equity Increase**
Just-in-time delivery of products, parts	Value equity	Co-op advertising support	Brand equity/ Relationship equity
Usage of dedicated logistics system for KAs only	Value equity/ Relationship equity	Additional merchandising assistance (POP, trade shows, plan-o-grams)	Brand equity/ Relationship equity
Expedited delivery of products or services at no extra charge	Value equity/ Relationship equity	National advertising campaign to build brand awareness, knowledge, image, preference, and purchase intentions	Brand equity
Operational linkages and EDI	Relationship equity	Direct marketing, internet, and sales promotion tie-ins with KA	Value equity/ Brand equity
		Links to supplier's website for direct referrals, customer service	Value equity/ Relationship equity

Figure 2. Marketing strategies to increase value, brand, and relationship equity.

relationship equity. Brand equity increases because awareness of Dell computers increases, and brand awareness is one important component of brand equity (Keller, 2008). Relationship equity would also increase as co-op advertising programs operate much like customer loyalty or affinity programs (Rust et al., 2000) in that, the more a company spends on a cooperative advertising budget, the more it qualifies for in terms of advertising allowance money, up to a predetermined limit. It therefore links one company (Intel) to another (Dell) through financial benefits (Rust et al., 2000, 2001). In some ways, co-op programs are also like special reward programs (Rust et al., 2000) for KA customers who spend enough on advertising to qualify for cooperative advertising dollars.

The strategies shown in Figure 2 clearly do not represent the entire range nor depth of strategic marketing decisions employed in KA programs. They are presented here as illustrative examples only to identify strategic options that will increase value, brand, and relationship equity in order to demonstrate their impact on the model. Further, they are provided as examples of commonly used KA program strategies or trade strategies (e.g. Belch & Belch, 2009; Ryals & Holt, 2007). The following section offers propositions on value equity, brand equity, and relationship equity and their effects on relationship commitment and trust.

Value, brand, and relationship equity: antecedents to commitment and trust

Value equity

In determining value, buyers evaluate what they are required to give up and what they receive in return (Zeithaml, 1988). KA managers may adjust their quality or prices (Ryals & Holt, 2007) as examples of strategic changes designed to influence these perceptions of value. For example, when a KA manager negotiates the price/quality trade-off with an account, the manager's ability to deliver more quality at a lower price will positively impact the buyer's perception of value. As the customer's perception of value increases, s/he will become more committed to the relationship. Buyers in a KA context will not seek to do business with sellers who are unable to provide real value; however, when real value is perceived, then KAs will be more committed to the relationship (Lemon et al., 2001). Additional support was noted earlier in that relationship commitment suggests that both parties have engaged in efforts and 'affirmative actions' in which they have staked something of value on the long-term continuance of the relationship (Gundlach et al., 1995). Thus, an increase in the perception of value received by one party should strengthen that party's commitment to the relationship. Value is the central component of building committed KA relationships. Therefore:

P1: Increases in value equity yield increases in relationship commitment.

Brand equity

A brand can be thought of as a promise from the seller to maintain certain quality levels (DelVecchio, 2000). KA managers must focus on the subjective evaluation of the offering to impact brand equity. These subjective evaluations are built above and beyond value equity perceptions (Lemon et al., 2001). For example, KA managers and selling firms that focus on practicing high ethical standards (Rust et al., 2004) or providing relevant information in a timely manner (Sengupta et al., 2000) will improve the customer's perception of the brand. These increased brand perceptions should lead to higher levels of buyer trust as both perceptions of integrity and reliability (e.g. Morgan & Hunt, 1994) will be positively impacted by such actions. The seller's integrity and reliability are both fundamental to building trust. These elements of trust are both positively impacted as customers come to realize that brand promises are consistently kept by the seller over time. Therefore:

P2: Increases in brand equity yield increases in trust.

Relationship equity

Unlike B2C research where relationship equity programs are added experiences to capture the customer's loyalty (e.g. frequent flyer programs), the KA management context is, by definition, focused on building relationships. KA managers focus most of their efforts on building and maintaining the important relationships under their control (Ryals & Holt, 2007; Sengupta et al., 2000). For example, strategic actions such as preferential treatment, transaction specific investments, and special recognition programs are all designed to cement the relationship with the buyer (Workman et al., 2003). The impact of these and other relational strategies is twofold. First, as KA managers work to build relationship equity, they will work to provide the consistent, dependable service and product quality that form the basis for customer trust (Sengupta et al., 2000). Second, as buyers begin to depend on KAs for greater levels of customer service and product line customization, their levels of commitment to the relationship grow (Workman et al., 2003). Therefore:

P3: Increases in relationship equity yield increases in trust.

P4: Increases in relationship equity yield increases in relationship commitment.

Trust: antecedent to relationship commitment

Consistent with previous research (Morgan & Hunt, 1994), trust will be a determinant of relationship commitment in the proposed strategic framework. This assertion follows other researchers (Achrol, 1991; Hrebiniak, 1974) that suggest people will commit themselves to maintain relationships built on trust because these relationships are so valuable. Moorman et al. (1992) found additional empirical support for the relationship between trust and commitment in the context of a service provider. Therefore:

P5: Increases in trust yield increases in relationship commitment.

KA performance: profitability and share of spend

KA performance has been defined previously as both a relational variable (e.g. relationship effectiveness, Sengupta et al., 2000) and as a financial outcome such as market performance or profitability (Homburg et al., 2002; Ryals & Holt, 2007). As noted earlier, however, the strategic framework proposed here positions commitment and trust as relational mediators and direct antecedents to KA performance. Therefore, KA performance will be assessed here using two financial measures: long-term profitability and share of customer spend.

Long-term profitability is used because some KAs may be unprofitable in the short term until revenue streams exceed account acquisition and set-up costs. Of course, some suppliers may be willing to accept zero profit contributions on KAs in the short term because of the ability to achieve economies of scale (Ryals & Holt, 2007). There is evidence that not all KAs are profitable (Cooper & Kaplan, 1991; van Raaij, Vernooij, & van Triest, 2003), which makes this outcome critical to monitor.

Another KA performance measure is share of spend. Share of spend represents the percentage of a customer's annual business garnered by a selling firm. It is analogous to market share but at the account level rather than the firm level. Homburg et al. (2002) used a number of market performance indicators in their research, one of which was market share over the last three years. A supplier's share of spend is important to KA performance because it was identified as one measure of the financial value in a KA management relationship (Ryals & Holt, 2007).

Trust, relationship commitment, and value equity: antecedents to KA performance

The model posits three direct antecedents to KA performance, two of which are relational mediators. The two relational mediators are trust and relationship commitment, and the other direct antecedent is value equity. First, the relationships between trust, relationship commitment, and performance are examined.

Trust and commitment

According to Workman et al. (2003), KA performance is dependent upon the quality of the relationship between the selling firm and its KA customer. Relationship quality or effectiveness is typically posited to be a function of antecedents such as trust (e.g. Homburg et al., 2002; Morgan & Hunt, 1994; Sengupta et al., 2000) and commitment (Dwyer et al., 1987; Morgan & Hunt, 1994). It is logical that, as commitment to a selling organization increases, the amount (and relative percentage) the customer purchases from that supplier should increase. As partners continue in a committed relationship, cross-selling is likely to occur along with increased customer penetration for new products (e.g. Dwyer et al., 1987). And as both trust and commitment grow and those revenue percentages continue to increase, it is likely that profitability will eventually increase as well. In a separate but related body of research, the link between loyalty and profitability is due partly to increased revenues as well as cost reductions (e.g. Berry, 1995; Reichheld & Sasser, 1990). Ryals and Holt (2007) emphasize the KA manager's focus on both increased revenues and decreased costs over time.

Further support is found in Workman et al. (2003) where KA management effectiveness (which included measures of trust and long-term relationship maintenance) was significantly, positively related to market performance, including a measure of market share. Market performance was then positively related to profitability. In addition, previous research found evidence that market performance indicators (e.g. market share, satisfaction, and loyalty) are positively related to financial performance (Anderson, Fornell, & Lehmann, 1994; Fornell, 1992), including profitability (Reichheld, 1996). Although there are exceptions (e.g. Reinartz & Kumar, 2000), there is conceptual and empirical evidence that organizations that enjoy long-term, committed relationships with their customers enjoy greater profitability than those with only short-term, transactional customer relationships (Morgan & Hunt, 1994; Reichheld, 1996; Reichheld & Sasser, 1990; Reichheld & Teal, 1996; Sheth & Parvatiyar, 1995). Both market share (a concept analogous to share of spend at the KA level) and profitability have been found to be related to relationship commitment and trust. Thus, KA performance, as measured by long-term profitability and share of spend, should be positively influenced by the level of KA relationship commitment and trust. Therefore:

> P6: Increases in relationship commitment yield increases in KA performance: (a) long-term profitability and (b) share of spend.

> P7: Increases in trust yield increases in KA performance: (a) long-term profitability and (b) share of spend.

Value equity

Given the central role that the exchange of value plays in building business relationships (Cannon & Homburg, 2001) and in serving as the foundation for building customer equity (Rust et al., 2000), the theoretical model specifies a direct relationship between value equity and KA performance. Anderson (1995, p. 348) suggests that, 'the essential purpose for a customer firm and supplier firm engaging in a collaborative relationship is to work together in ways that add value or reduce cost in the exchange between the firms.' Specifically in the KA context, Ryals and Holt (2007) explore the relationships between revenue enhancements and cost cutting (both fundamental to building value) and their outcome – KA performance. Their study suggests a direct relationship between value and account profitability.

Value is also noted with importance in the customer equity literature. Value equity holds a place of prominence among the three equity drivers (Rust et al., 2000) and only value equity is sufficient by itself as a cause for establishing and maintaining business relationships (Lemon et al., 2001). Value equity, as previously mentioned, is defined as the customer's objective evaluation of what is received compared to what is given up in an exchange. Marketing managers attempt to positively influence these perceptions of quality, price and convenience (Rust et al., 2000). 'Value equity matters to most customers most of the time', according to Lemon et al. (2001, p. 23) and will be most important when complex purchase decisions, long-term commitments, and large sums of money are involved as is common with KA relationships. This direct path in the proposed theoretical model highlights the central role of value in business relationships and the importance of value equity above and beyond that of brand or relationship equity.

The inclusion of a direct path indicates a partial mediation between value equity and KA performance through relationship commitment. The nature of this partially mediated relationship further implies that performance is impacted by elements of value above and beyond those transmitted by relationship commitment. These additional impacts on performance may be the result of customer pressure to reduce transaction costs and to extract value (Ryals & Holt, 2007).

Supplier firms attempting to capture value from key accounts identify the profitability of the relationship (Niraj, Gupta, & Narasimhan, 2001; Ryals, 2005) and market-based outcomes such as share of spend as essential outcomes of interest (Homburg et al., 2002). This focus on profits and share of spend further links these important performance outcomes to the management of delivering and extracting value from KAs. As the customer's perceptions of value equity increase, it is expected that both profitability and share of spend will also increase for the KA. Therefore:

P8: Increases in value equity yield increases in KA performance: (a) long-term profitability and (b) share of spend.

Discussion

As companies seek to strengthen customer relationships and obtain greater value from their KAs, the importance of having a strategic framework for KA performance increases. The conceptual model proposed here represents an initial attempt at providing a theoretical model for understanding and managing KA relational outcomes and financial performance. At the same time, limitations of this model must be acknowledged in order to guide and foster further research in the area. The strategic decisions presented here were limited in scope in that they all represented marketing actions that would have a positive impact on equity. The model did not consider strategic activities that might not contribute to improvements in value, brand, or relationship equity (e.g. an unexplained increase in pricing). While acknowledging that circumstances sometimes force companies to make business decisions that adversely affect customers, it seemed logical to start first with a conceptual model in which the goal was to increase customer equity. In addition, no research propositions were developed for the relationships between the various marketing strategies and the customer equity drivers. Figure 2 provides examples of common strategic decisions and their likely increase on each specific type of equity. However, no attempt is made to fully articulate all KA strategic decisions from part one of the framework, nor to fully propose these relationships. The contributions associated with the proposed strategic framework are not related to specific strategic decisions, rather to the development of a framework to guide decision making. Finally, while this model is proposed and supported with theoretical arguments, future research is needed to provide empirical support.

Contributions

Despite its drawbacks, this research adds to the KA literature in several ways. First, it represents a managerially practical and comprehensive strategic framework for managing KA performance. Built on customer equity theory, the model suggests that KA managers make strategic marketing decisions that build value along one (or more) of three paths. These three paths guide decisions regarding value, brand, and relationship equity. Thus, account managers can focus on the equity drivers that are most important to their customers (recognizing that the importance of the three equity drivers may vary across

KAs), and direct marketing and other organizational resources where they will have the most impact. Lemon et al. (2001, p. 25) suggest that, 'once a firm understands the critical drivers of customer equity for its industry and for its key customers, the firm can respond to its customer and the marketplace with strategies that maximize its performance'. The model proposed here goes a step further in that it identifies the (relational) links between the strategies and the KA performance outcomes.

Second, this study links the theoretical underpinnings of the customer equity literature with that of the relationship marketing literature – an integration that seems essential in B2B relationships, especially in a KA context. The central focus of relationship marketing models, commitment and trust, is at the heart of this model in that these two variables mediate the relationship between value equity, brand equity, and relationship equity, and KA performance. Conceptually, this integrative model provides scholars a guiding framework for future research in KA performance. In fact, theory building in all three areas – KAs, relationship marketing, and customer equity – can potentially be advanced through empirical validation of the model.

Third, the level of analysis suggested in this research is important to consider. As previously mentioned, most empirical KA studies either capture data within a single firm and attempt to explain variance across KA managers (e.g. Sengupta et al., 2000) or capture data across multiple firms and attempt to explain variance across companies (Workman et al., 2003). While these two differing levels of analysis are useful for answering their own questions (e.g. how to structure account management at the organizational level or how to select/train account managers at the individual level), they leave a gap for account managers who must function at a third level – the account level. This third level of analysis has been employed in recent empirical studies. Palmatier et al. (2007) based an empirical study at the 'exchange level' and argued that this is the fundamental level for marketing scholarship. The exchange level of analysis allows for strategic planning at the account level and incorporates decisions regarding the firm and individual KA managers into a single model. The theoretical combination of the organizational and personal levels opens opportunities for an expansion of our knowledge at a level that is most useful for managers. This study argues that an exchange-level strategic framework is one that is most appropriate and most useful to managers.

Fourth, KA managers and companies that deploy KA managers make some implicit assumptions about the desires of the customer to be in a relationship with the selling firm. These assumptions may not turn out to be true in all cases (Piercy & Lane, 2003). When business customers seek to maintain a transactional relationship and sellers seek to build long-term relationships, obvious conflicts are likely to arise. Piercy and Lane (2003) rightly argue that this mismatch in goals can make the adoption of traditional KA management practices an unwise choice with every account. The strategic framework proposed here is well suited to address this conflict in goals between buyers and sellers in that it allows for account-level strategic decisions to reflect a key customer's preference for transactional relations. In this case, value equity could focus on limited services and price discounts for large volumes, brand equity could focus on minimizing or sharing advertising support, and relationship equity could be limited to investments that improve transactional efficiency. The proposed framework is robust enough to handle a variety of account management situations – even accounts that desire limited levels of commitment.

Finally, this model provides KA managers support as they secure resources from across the selling organization. Competing for limited resources is difficult but important for KA managers. The nature of their role as account managers requires that they serve as intermediaries between their accounts and their company. This boundary spanning role typically involves securing resources to serve their accounts (Napolitano, 1997). By adopting this customer equity framework, account managers' goals are better aligned with corporate goals to build customer equity across all levels of accounts.

Future research

A logical first step in solidifying the usefulness of this theoretical model would be to test the research propositions. A thorough test of the theoretical model's structure would be helpful in providing support for the links between the three customer equity drivers, the relational outcomes KAs desire, and the KA performance variables.

A search for boundary conditions on the framework should also produce additional theoretical and practical insights. These moderators may come in one of two forms, either control variables on the relational and performance outcomes or conceptual moderators. Control variables such as competitive intensity, channel power, and length of relationship have all been investigated in previous KA studies (e.g. Workman et al., 2003). This list of potential control variables is not exhaustive but serves as a useful starting point. A search for this type of control variable will help to isolate the explanatory power of the theoretical model.

A search for the second type of moderator should prove more interesting. These moderators determine the conditions under which the strategic model best predicts relational and financial performance. One potential area for moderation in the model is the combination of equity strategies. There may be situations when the different equity drivers interact with each other. Rust et al. (2004) found empirical evidence of distinctions among the three customer equity drivers and their consequences, but did not test their potential interactions. These interactions should be of interest in future studies. For example, it may be that the relationship between relationship equity and its consequents (trust and commitment) will be weakened by low value equity given the primary role of value equity in establishing profitable relationships. Therefore, searches for this and other interactions in the model should help scholars better understand the relative value of each driver in a KA context.

Researchers have introduced a number of relational mediators into the Morgan and Hunt (1994) framework, including cooperation (Anderson & Narus, 1990; Dwyer et al., 1987) and functionality of conflict (Anderson & Narus, 1990; Dwyer et al., 1987). A search for additional mediators should aid managers in particular as they stand to benefit from additional knowledge of important paths to KA financial performance.

Further research is called for that explores specific KA strategies to influence each of the three value drivers as previously noted. This explication of specific KA strategies for each driver would best be carried out in longitudinal, empirical studies where evidence of the effects of these strategies could be measured and evaluated over time.

References

Achrol, R. (1991). Evolution of the marketing organization: New forms for turbulent environments. *Journal of Marketing, 55*(4), 77–93.

Anderson, E.W., Fornell, C., & Lehmann, D.R. (1994). Customer satisfaction, market share, and profitability: Findings from Sweden. *Journal of Marketing, 58*(July), 53–66.

Anderson, J.C. (1995). Relationships in business markets: Exchange episodes, value creation and their empirical assessment. *Journal of the Academy of Marketing Science, 23*(Fall), 346–350.

Anderson, J.C., & Narus, J.A. (1990). A model of distributor firm and manufacturer firm working partnerships. *Journal of Marketing, 54*(January), 42–58.

Belch, G., & Belch, M. (2009). *Advertising and promotion: An integrated marketing communications perspective*. New York: McGraw-Hill/Irwin.

Berry, L.L. (1995). Relationship marketing of services: Growing interest, emerging perspectives. *Journal of the Academy of Marketing Science, 23*(4), 236–245.

Boles, J.S., Barksdale, H.C., Jr, & Johnson, J.T. (1996). What national account decision makers would tell salespeople about building relationships. *Journal of Business and Industrial Marketing, 11*(2), 6–19.

Cannon, J.P., & Homburg, C. (2001). Buyer–supplier relationships and customer firm costs. *Journal of Marketing, 65*(January), 29–43.

Cooper, R., & Kaplan, R.C. (1991). Profit priorities from ABC. *Harvard Business Review, 69*(3), 130–134.

DelVecchio, D. (2000). Moving beyond fit: The role of brand portfolio characteristics in consumer evaluations of brand reliability. *Journal of Product and Brand Management, 9*(7), 457–471.

Dishman, P., & Nitse, P.S. (1998). National accounts revisited: New lessons from recent investigations. *Industrial Marketing Management, 27*(January), 1–9.

Dwyer, R.F., Schurr, P.H., & Oh, S. (1987). Developing buyer–seller relationships. *Journal of Marketing, 51*(April), 11–27.

Fornell, C.G. (1992). A national customer satisfaction barometer: The Swedish experience. *Journal of Marketing, 56*(January), 6–21.

Gundlach, G.T., Achrol, R.S., & Mentzer, J.T. (1995). The structure of commitment. *Journal of Marketing, 59*(January), 78–92.

Homburg, C., Workman, J.P., Jr, & Jensen, O. (2000). Fundamental changes in marketing organization: The movement toward a customer-focused organizational structure. *Journal of the Academy of Marketing Science, 28*(4), 459–478.

Homburg, C., Workman, J.P., Jr, & Jensen, O. (2002). A configurational perspective on key account management. *Journal of Marketing, 66*(April), 38–60.

Hrebiniak, L.G. (1974). Effects of job level and participation on employee attitudes and perceptions of influence. *Academy of Management Journal, 17*(4), 649–662.

Jones, E., Brown, S.P., Zoltners, A.A., & Weitz, B.A. (2005). The changing environment of selling and sales management. *Journal of Personal Selling and Sales Management, 25*(2), 105–111.

Keller, K.L. (2008). *Strategic brand management: Building, measuring, and managing brand equity*. New York: Prentice-Hall.

Kuratko, D.F., Montagno, R.V., & Hornsby, J.S. (1990). Developing an intrapreneurial assessment instrument for an effective corporate entrepreneurial environment. *Strategic Management Journal, 11*(Summer), 49–58.

Leigh, T.W., & Marshall, G.W. (2001). Research priorities in sales strategy and performance. *Journal of Personal Selling and Sales Management, 21*(2), 83–94.

Lemon, K.N., Rust, R.T., & Zeithaml, V.A. (2001). What drives customer equity? *Marketing Management, 10*(Spring), 20–25.

Montgomery, D.B., & Yip, G.S. (2000). The challenge of global customer management. *Marketing Management, 9*(4), 22–29.

Moorman, C., Deshpande, R., & Zaltman, G. (1993). Factors affecting trust in market research relationships. *Journal of Marketing, 57*(January), 81–101.

Moorman, C., Zaltman, G., & Deshpande, R. (1992). Relationships between providers and users of marketing research: The dynamics of trust within and between organizations. *Journal of Marketing Research, 29*(August), 314–329.

Morgan, R.M., & Hunt, S.D. (1994). The commitment–trust theory of relationship marketing. *Journal of Marketing, 58*(July), 20–38.

Napolitano, L. (1997). Customer–supplier partnering: A strategy whose time has come. *Journal of Personal Selling & Sales Management, 17*(4), 1–8.

Niraj, R., Gupta, M., & Narasimhan, C. (2001). Customer profitability in a supply chain. *Journal of Marketing, 65*(July), 1–16.

Noble, S.M., & Phillips, J. (2004). Relationship hindrance: Why would consumers not want a relationship with a retailer? *Journal of Retailing, 80*(4), 289–303.

Palmatier, R.W., Dant, R.P., & Grewal, D. (2007). A comparative longitudinal analysis of theoretical perspectives of interorganizational relationship performance. *Journal of Marketing, 71*(4), 172–194.

Piercy, N.F., & Lane, N. (2003). Transformation of the traditional sales force: Imperatives for intelligence, interface and integration. *Journal of Marketing Management, 19*(5–6), 563–582.

Reichheld, F.F. (1996). *The loyalty effect: The hidden force behind growth, profits, and lasting value.* Cambridge, MA: Harvard Business School Press.

Reichheld, F.F., & Sasser, E.W. (1990). Zero defections: Quality comes to services. *Harvard Business Review, 68*(September/October), 105–111.

Reichheld, F.F., & Teal, T. (1996). *The loyalty effect.* Boston, MA: Harvard Business School Press.

Reinartz, W.J., & Kumar, V. (2000). On the profitability of long-life customers in a noncontractual setting: An empirical investigation and implications for marketing. *Journal of Marketing, 64*(October), 17–35.

Rust, R.T., Lemon, K.N., & Zeithaml, V.A. (2001). Where should the next marketing dollar go? *Marketing Management, 10*(3), 25–28.

Rust, R.T., Lemon, K.N., & Zeithaml, V.A. (2004). Return on marketing: Using customer equity to focus marketing strategy. *Journal of Marketing, 68*(January), 109–127.

Rust, R.T., Zeithaml, V.A., & Lemon, K.N. (2000). *Driving customer equity: How customer lifetime value is reshaping corporate strategy.* New York: The Free Press.

Ryals, L.J. (2005). Making customer relationship management work: The measurement and profitable management of customer relationships. *Journal of Marketing, 69*(4), 252–261.

Ryals, L.J. (2006). Profitable relationships with key customers: How suppliers manage pricing and customer risk. *Journal of Strategic Marketing, 14*(2), 101–113.

Ryals, L.J., & Holt, S. (2007). Creating and capturing value in KAM relationships. *Journal of Strategic Marketing, 15*(4), 403–420.

Ryals, L.J., & Rogers, B. (2007). Key account planning: Benefits, barriers and best practice. *Journal of Strategic Marketing, 15*(2–3), 209–222.

Schultz, R.J., & Evans, K. (2002). Strategic collaborative communication by key account representatives. *Journal of Personal Selling & Sales Management, 22*(1), 23–31.

Sengupta, S., Krapfel, R.E., & Pusateri, M.A. (1997a). The strategic sales force. *Marketing Management, 6*(Summer), 29–34.

Sengupta, S., Krapfel, R.E., & Pusateri, M.A. (1997b). Switching costs in key account relationships. *Journal of Personal Selling & Sales Management, 17*(4), 9–16.

Sengupta, S., Krapfel, R.E., & Pusateri, M.A. (2000). An empirical investigation of key account salesperson effectiveness. *Journal of Personal Selling & Sales Management, 20*(4), 253–261.

Shapiro, B.P., & Moriarty, R.T. (1980). *National account management. Marketing Science Institute working paper no. 80-104.* Cambridge, MA: Marketing Science Institute.

Shapiro, B.P., & Moriarty, R.T. (1984). *Organizing the national account force. Marketing Science Institute working paper no. 84-101.* Cambridge, MA: Marketing Science Institute.

Sheth, J.N., & Parvatiyar, A. (1995). Relationship in consumer markets: Antecedents and consequences. *Journal of the Academy of Marketing Science, 23*(4), 255–271.

Smith, J.B., & Barclay, D.W. (1997). The effect of organizational differences and trust on the effectiveness of selling relationships. *Journal of Marketing, 61*(January), 3–21.

Van Raaij, E.M., Vernooij, J.J.A., & van Triest, S. (2003). The implementation of customer profitability analysis: A case study. *Industrial Marketing Management, 32*(7), 573–583.

Vogel, V., Evanschitzky, H., & Ramaseshan, B. (2008). Customer equity drivers and future sales. *Journal of Marketing, 72*(November), 98–108.

Workman, J.P., Jr, Homburg, C., & Jensen, O. (2003). Intraorganizational determinants of key account management effectiveness. *Journal of the Academy of Marketing Science, 31*(1), 3–21.

Wotruba, T.R., & Castleberry, S.B. (1993). Job analysis and hiring practices for national account marketing positions. *Journal of Personal Selling & Sales Management, 13*(3), 49–65.

Zeithaml, V.A. (1988). Consumer perceptions of price, quality, and value: A means–end model and synthesis of evidence. *Journal of Marketing, 52*(July), 2–22.

The implications of lean operations for sales strategy: from sales-force to marketing-force

Niall Piercy and Nick Rich

Lean operating principles are based on the systems of Toyota Japan. Companies around the world, in all sectors of the economy, now embrace these approaches to improve quality, cost and productivity. Different purchasing and sourcing practices in lean organisations mean that winning sales from them requires major changes to sales strategy and practice. This process has not been fully explored. Serving lean customers, who demand complete transparency across the supplying organisation and focus on capability not cost, has proven problematic for traditional sales departments. Further, as supplying organisations themselves become lean (this transformation being a result and requirement of selling to a lean company), organisational redesign extends from operations into sales. This paper illustrates the shifts needed in sales approach and strategy in selling to, and subsequently, becoming a lean business. The role of this future-sales-force is considered in relation to its shift towards a marketing-orientated rather than sales-push strategy.

Introduction

The adoption of lean or Japanese approaches to operations and production management has become a common practice among European and American manufacturing and service businesses (Womack & Jones, 2003). Well established within the field of operations management, the implications of lean change for the non-operational areas of the business are less well understood (Piercy & Morgan, 1997). A key part of lean operation is a shift in the nature of supply relationships – moving from transactional cost-buying to long run partnership. This change requires far more than the basic relationship-management approaches currently identified in the supply chain or sales literatures (Hines, 1994). The requirements that are placed on a company seeking to supply a lean organisation, and as a result the role and tasks of the sales team, are fundamentally different to those encountered in supplying a traditionally organised business or in moving from one-off to repeat-relationship style account management (Lamming, 1996). For the sales manager, encountering a lean organisation can be a troubling and uncertain experience when faced with clients who no longer buy solely based on price, will not accept discounting, expect full transparency of every suppliers' costing, demand net-zero price increases and assess the company on all its abilities, from product quality to the track record of the senior executives. There remains almost no academic guidance on how dealing with a lean business will change the nature of the sales–purchaser relationship.

To maintain a relationship with a lean customer, the company must itself embrace lean change in principles practice (Wincell, 2003). Lean improvement may be driven by the operational area of the business but the changes are at a systems or organisation-wide level, touching every area of the business (Liker, 2003; Liker & Hoseus, 2007). The requirements for human resources, marketing, sales and finance that are created by lean change programmes have been largely overlooked (Balle & Balle, 2005). The internal transformations required in sales affect the internal organisation of the department and how they are required to work with other areas of the business, from internal process mapping of administrative tasks such as placing a sales order, to the co-location of sales staff onto production line cells to improve product knowledge.

In this paper we set out to analyse the challenges for the sales force in encountering and seeking to serve a lean organisation. We then consider the trickle-down effects of lean change inside the supplying company and the issues they will encounter. Throughout the change process, the sales force is pulled away from production-/sales-push approaches (selling their existing products to customers based on sales-discounting) towards offering bespoke services that the buying customers inherently want and need. Over time this process can transform the sales-force into a marketing-force. The implications for the role of sales in the organisation of this shift are discussed.

The background of lean thinking

By the 1970s the rise of Japanese manufacturing expertise was increasingly obvious (Altshuler, Anderson, Jones, Roos, & Womack, 1986). The ability to deliver products of higher quality and at lower cost than European and North American manufacturers fuelled Japanese domination in key sectors of the economy from automotive to electronics (Hayes & Wheelwright, 1984; Monden, 1983).

The success of Japanese companies was powered by operational and organisational systems that were fundamentally different to the mass-production, scientifically managed approaches of western businesses. Developed in the aftermath of World War II, the methods of Toyota were driven by resource shortages and the need to maximise outputs from production. Their investigation of western production methodologies suggested massive waste and inefficiency, capital intensity and poor employment engagement (Deming, 1982a, 1982b). Focusing on finding ways to remove these wastes and inefficiency, a new operational system emerged (Ohno, 1988). Core to this approach was a systems or process-based, holistic approach to organisation. This included a focus on coordinating all product flows, from raw materials inputs to final customers (Monden, 1983; Shingo, 1981, 1988). There was a belief that no one, single company could achieve quality–cost–productivity outcomes in isolation – only when their entire supply chain, providing all resource inputs into the company was managed, could these requirements be met (Monden, 1983; Ohno, 1988; Shingo, 1981, 1988).

The most extensive investigation of Japanese, lean style production remains the International Motor Vehicle Programme (IMVP), based at MIT in the late 1990s. This reported a gap of 2:1 in productivity and 100:1 in quality of the vehicles produced in Toyota Japan versus the West (Womack, Jones, & Roos, 1990). This revelation fostered interest in Toyota style approaches and the development of methodologies for replicating their management system. This system became established as lean production. Proposing key principles for lean change, Womack and Jones (1996) fuelled a massive uptake in lean transformation across the western world. Manufacture and service, private and public businesses are now embracing lean approaches. Focusing both on internal operational improvement and also on supply chain integration, these efforts are shifting the nature and content of exchanges between companies and their supply chain (Womack & Jones, 2003).

The changing nature of sales–purchaser relationships

The practice of supply chain management has come to describe the coordinated management of the many different companies involved in producing a product, from raw materials to end customer (Chopra, Lovejoy, & Yano, 2004). Interest in the concept has steadily increased since the 1980s when firms saw the benefits of forming long term, collaborative relationships with their supplying companies (Lummus & Vokurka, 1999). Purchasing through the market mechanisms, adversarial relationships emerge between buyer and seller, each seeking to maximise their individual utility – for sales, achieving the maximum price/sales possible; for the purchaser, paying the lowest price possible. The adversarial nature of the relationship is problematic for both parties – each sacrificing quality for cost reduction (Dyer, 1997; Fujimoto, 1999; Hines, 1994; Smitka, 1991). Under lean production, rather than source from whichever supplier was cheapest, often buying in bulk to secure discounts, companies form close, recurring and long term relationships with small groups of suppliers who are expected to consistently offer them better quality (Hines, 1994; Lamming, 1996). Benefits of collaborative relations include better information exchange, quality improvement, cost reduction and co-development of new products, all offering major improvement gains for companies (Chandra & Kumar, 2000; MacBeth & Ferguson, 1994; Merli, 1991).

Gaining and maintaining this relationship, the primary role of the sales group, is much harder and more intense than cost-based sales, traditional key account management or completing supplier evaluation systems due to the wide range of criteria used by the lean company (Toyota, 1997). The diffusion of lean approaches across the economy necessitates a better examination of these changes.

The spread of lean approaches

While the first stages of lean change focus on operational areas within the organisation as lean change extends the requirements for supply inputs rapidly change, and as a result, so too do the behaviours and activities of staff seeking to sell to the lean business. The spread of lean operational approaches to every sector of the economy is well under way (Womack & Jones, 2003). This process of diffusion has been through direct investment in the West by Japanese organisations, change in organisations serving these Japanese transplants and replication efforts across the economy as companies see the benefits on offer from lean improvement (Anderson Consulting, 1992, 1994).

The first wave of Japanese lean entrants was limited to the automotive sector. As these companies established supply chains in the domestic economies of Europe and the United States the requirements placed on the suppliers into these companies shifted purchasing, supply and sales practices. While western businesses sought to improve supply standards by auditing and removing poorly performing suppliers, leaving them to improve on their own, Japanese companies pushed lean practices into their suppliers, educating them and evolving their businesses into the lean model (Anderson Consulting, 1992, 1994).

Embracing lean change these suppliers themselves found the need to push lean approaches into their own supply base. Lean adoption by one large, focal organisation leads to a trickle-down effect through the supply chain as companies selling to lean businesses themselves undergo lean transformation (Wincell, 2003) (shown in Figure 1). As several hundred tier one supply companies undergo lean adoption, over time their suppliers will too see lean development, leading to several thousand companies seeing benefits from alignment with a single focal organisation.

Elsewhere, the impacts of lean change are being studied and emulated. Major reports on the state of western business have called for the need for manufacturing and services to adopt lean change (Egan, 1998; Jones & Mitchell, 2006; Shaw, Lengyel, & Ferre, 2004). Evidence suggests these calls are being heeded by companies and a fundamental shift is occurring in the organising principles of western business (EEF, 2007).

Despite its automotive origins, lean approaches have been embraced across the economy as a whole. Lean approaches have spread downwards through automotive components suppliers, to their raw materials suppliers, and back up the value chain into areas as diverse as aerospace and pharmaceuticals. Companies like Airbus or Rolls-Royce, Johnson and Johnson, Novartis and GlaxoSmithKline have all embraced lean approaches (Womack & Jones 2003). Japanese entrants to western markets are no longer limited to the automotive sector. Toyota is pushing into many areas as distinct as house building, aerospace, biotechnology and mobile technologies, kick-starting similar trickle-down effects (Toyota, 2008).

Beyond manufacturing, retailers such as Tesco and Walmart have converted to lean based purchasing (Jones, 2001). Large scale civil engineering companies like Bechtel, Carillion and Transport 4 London have changed their dealings with sales forces as they rationalise supply bases and work closer with lean suppliers (Egan, 1998). In the public sector, the National Health Service has become one of the largest adopters of lean

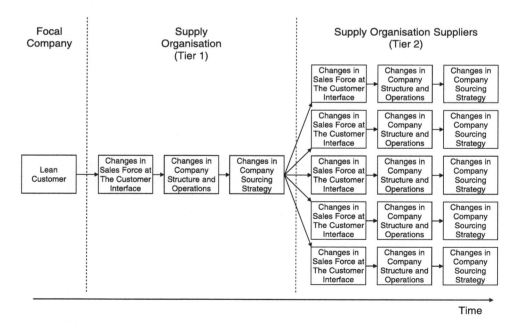

Figure 1.   The lean trickle-down effect.

approaches, with an increasing focus on changing how they spend their £20 billion annual procurement budget, systematically changing how they deal with sales force representatives (Jones & Mitchell, 2006).

As these large companies adopt lean procurement strategies, their suppliers, and their suppliers' suppliers, all replicate and emulate lean methodologies (the only way to deliver the quality demands of a lean customer in the long run is to ensure your own internal processes are lean, and as a consequence your supply inputs) (Wincell, 2003). Sales forces serving these businesses have had to change their attitudes and approaches to suit the lean businesses requirements.

Lean sales force

Dealing with lean requirements in sales may be an increasingly unavoidable issue for sales strategy (Monden, 1997). As companies rationalise their supply base, often from thousands to hundreds of suppliers, close working relationships, often in a lean mould, are becoming a strategic requirement to win business (Helper, 1991; Nishiguchi, 1994). For the sales team engaging with the lean organisation there are many benefits on offer. The long term nature of the client relationship supports guaranteed orders over time, providing a reassurance lacking when continually chasing sales and seeking new clients (Sako, 1992). It is unusual for lean companies to switch suppliers once a contract is underway, providing a long term stability for the company (MacBeth & Ferguson, 1994). The requirements of the relationship will be clearly and openly specified at the beginning of a sales/supply contract and adhered to, without the game playing and political positioning common in many negotiations (Cox, Lonsdale, Sanderson, & Watson, 2004). Demand patterns over the period of the contract will be clearly communicated long in advance of actual demand. Rather than continually scrabbling to increase volumes or absorb stocking costs in off-peak times, long run predicted demand data are provided for planning purposes (Monden, 1998). When facing shortages under an economic downturn, many non-lean companies, with large stocks of supplies on hand, are suspending all contracts with no restart date – providing major problems for sales and supply teams. Lean producers, without such stocks, are maintaining production at reduced levels, ensuring some level of sales are maintained (Rowley, 2008).

Despite extensive investigation of the requirements lean methodologies place on the internal workings of the company (Schonberger, 1986; Suzaki, 1987), and also on the supply chain that supplies this company (Hines, 1994; Lamming, 1996), the implications for the sales team, the key interface between the lean company and the inbound suppliers, has been entirely overlooked in existing research. The fundamentally different expectations and requirements placed on the sales team in the lean supply chain have not been identified or analysed. Lean approaches with long run partnership do not diminish the role of sales. Even though less direct selling is required, the role of the sales force is heightened not diminished (Kurogane, 1993; Monden, 1997). However, the new tasks they must complete are unfamiliar for the traditional sales force and have yet to be properly examined.

Research methodology

To analyse the changing role and requirements of sales under lean sourcing, the authors undertook primary and secondary research.

Secondary materials reviewed included literature as well as source materials from Japanese organisations. This included materials from Toyota Japan that specify Toyota's requirements for supply chain inputs (such as Toyota's *Supplier's guide for doing business with Toyota* (Toyota, 1997), *Toyota supplier policy* (Toyota, 2009) and *Toyota logistics manual* (Toyota, 1998)).

To examine the sales force role in more detail, the role of the sales force in western companies selling to Japanese transplants in the United Kingdom is analysed with primary investigation. The authors compiled 10 years of data from five major research projects that examined, and guided, automotive supplier change and development as they sought to sell to lean companies. These projects involved interviews with marketing, sales, production and operations personnel, customer interviews, observations of fulfilment processes and action-research over a 10 year period with nearly 100 suppliers in Europe (shown in Table 1). Lean change is now embraced in all sectors of the economy but the exemplar organisations, where the greatest changes have occurred, remain Japanese managed companies. Investigating these organisations provides a view on the future state of western lean emulators as their lean change programmes embrace new supply chain and sourcing strategies. First a narrative outline of the process of change to sales strategy and approach in selling to a lean company is provided in an in-depth case analysis. Following this, the key changes required from the sales force in selling to lean companies are presented.

The Nissan NX96 project

The shifts in sourcing approach, and the requirements this places on sales can be illustrated with the Nissan NX96 project, a £960m investment to establish an assembly plant in northern England in the 1990s. Faced with the challenge of using a European supply base, with far lower quality and reliability standards, and used to distant-transactional relationships, Nissan established a project to transform European suppliers to world class levels in a four year period. This became the largest, and still most successful, supplier transformation project in the automotive industry, bringing together the sales and operations teams of supply companies to transform their businesses.

The first stage of the project involved bringing in the sales teams of potential suppliers and briefing them on the expectations and requirements of what they had to be able to deliver. This included a wide range of performance data stating exactly what each team had to achieve in terms of quality, cost and capability (shown in Table 2). This transparent approach was a revelation for European suppliers. Clearly stating the quality, cost, delivery and management expectations in this manner was the first time any automotive company had shared so much with external sales teams.

Sales were left under no illusion that traditional sales methods – discounting on volume to win business – would not be an option. Companies were briefed on the wide range of metrics that would be used to determine if they received contracts. This included many fundamental shifts. First, a need to improve quality standards – traditional percentage failure rates were to be replaced with more stringent parts-per-million failure rates applied to all levels of the product (even packaging and labelling had to be correct). At the time European levels of quality were around 1400 PPM failure at tier one and 4000 at tier two, compared to 5 PPM and 400 PPM rates at Toyota Japan. An extensive auditing and reporting system for quality defects was pushed into each supplying company. Second, supplier companies were set for much tighter delivery schedules (from days, to times of day, to ultimately half-hour slots to feed production – at a time when western companies would accept $+/-2$ days as on-time delivery).

In addition, the cost-pricing relationship in selling to Nissan was also very different to traditional sales approaches. Sales were briefed that the prices they would set would no

Table 1. Research sample.

Project	Project description	Number of suppliers	Number of supply/ sales organisations	Sectors	Purchasing companies
World Class Supplier Learning Group, Welsh Development Agency	Working with suppliers trying to understand Nissan requirements	12	7 tier one (large) and 5 tier two suppliers (SME)	Component, plastics, tools, metals	Nissan (NX96 Project)
3-Day Car EPSRC Project	Research project to improve flow of materials in supply chain	12	6 tier one and 6 tier two suppliers	Raw materials, component, systems	Nissan, Toyota, Honda, Ford, Vauxhall
EPSRC LEAP Lean Processing Programme	Improve raw materials flow	23	7 tier one, 4 service centre, 12 end customers	Metals industry	Nissan, Toyota, Honda, Ford, Vauxhall
SCDP Supply Chain Development Programme Industry Sponsored Programme	Industry learning group on Japanese style supply requirements	19	12 tier one, 6 tier two, 1 aftermarket, end customers	Automotive component, FMCG companies, transport companies, telecommunications	Best practice of Nissan/Toyota
UK Supplier Association Programme	Improve performance of supply companies	24	17 tier one, 5 tier two, 2 tier three	Component, general engineering, major systems, raw material	Toyota, Rover

Table 2.   Nissan NX96 project: expectations of supplying organisations.

Item	Unit	1993	1994	1995	1996
Quality	Parts-per-million	250	180	90	50
Costing approach	Suppliers using open-book	60%	70%	80%	90%
Delivery	On-time delivery	92%	94%	96%	98%
Design defect	Suppliers meeting standard	85%	90%	95%	100%
Management	Partnership requirements met	40%	60%	80%	90%

longer be the established cost plus margin less discount approach. Nissan expected totally open book costing – each sales team would need to show the prices of all components and production of their parts – and a fair market price would be paid. Sales had to demonstrate their company's ability to improve continually the cost position. In common with Japanese sourcing, net-zero-annual cost increases were accepted – the price was fixed for the life of the contract and any increases in sourcing costs or inflation were expected to be absorbed by the supplier through improvement operations. In addition, Nissan would not pay for any modifications requested to the product over its lifetime (such as adding a mount to absorb noise on a radiator or later design changes). This was particularly unsettling for sales teams – a common approach in automotive sales had been to bid for business below the cost of production and then impose very large charges for such design modifications to recoup costs.

The nature of product specifications also changed. Whereas sales were used to going to a company and being issued a blueprint and told to quote for it, Nissan briefed them in a different manner. Sales were issued with performance targets and specified prices for a part that had to be designed and delivered (such as an air conditioning unit, that can chill from 18–30 degrees, in a cavity of 6" × 8" × 4" at £20/unit cost).

The sales teams for each company had to demonstrate the capability of the organisation. This included proving the management competency of the business – providing the curricula vitae of senior management; showing full accounts to show their financial position and solvency; a commitment to people and resource development; proving that the company was self-sufficient (not dependent on one key contract), had sound environmental planning, had annual improvement plans in place and were committed to developing their own supply base.

Many of these skills, required for any sales teams in selling to Nissan, were uncomfortable and unfamiliar to the sales staff of the time. The traditional mindset of selling products on cost had to be broken. A commitment on the part of sales, and the wider business, to commit to partnership was required. Sales teams were required to work across the business as a whole, much more closely with operational teams to communicate product specifications two-way, learning more about their products and going out to their own supply base to develop competencies.

Over the four year period the UK supply base was radically transformed. By the end of the project 200 UK suppliers were contributing 85% of the car to world-class supply standards, with only six development engineers in Nissan, sales teams were responsible for leading and driving change inside their own organisations.

The changing role of sales: the customer interface

Across all the transformation projects undertaken over the five research projects, several key themes emerged. At the customer interface several distinct issues were apparent.

Price

The biggest change for most sales forces concerns the end of discounting and price based competition for contracts. The dominant positioning tool for sales strategy becomes the competence and capability of the broader firm and not an ability to undercut rivals to win business. Lean organisations demand full open book costing – examining the full production cost in terms of materials and labour for every part they buy to determine a fair market price, not cost-plus-profit, which was set for the lifetime of the contract.

The prospect of open book costing terrified the UK sales teams. Despite this, no company walked away from working with the Japanese. The benefits of finding a long run client, in a growth area (the only large scale new plants opening were Japanese), when other areas of their businesses were declining were powerful lures to this methodology. In adopting open book costing, the biggest issue was customers' interest in the overhead costing process – Japanese companies were only willing to pay for their direct costs. European companies had not previously had to separate their overheads in this manner.

Lean organisations will expect net zero price increases and will not even accept price rises based on inflation. In addition, any modifications to the product or service over the life of the contract will not receive any additional payment. Supplying companies are expected to improve continually the efficiency of their operations through the life of the contract to absorb inflationary or other cost increases. All cost improvements are expected to be capability based (through removing materials and weight without negatively impacting product performance) and not based on labour cuts or off shoring as either activity removes the ability of the company to improve continually performance over time, a key competence required to win business with a lean producer. The first reaction of UK sales teams to these requirements was a general confusion about how to improve at the same speed as costs were going up. In-depth discussions with the Japanese purchasing companies on a one-on-one basis to help them understand the need for the approach and to train them on improvement approaches (such as process mapping or workplace redesign) took place.

The sales team in a lean company will also face challenges – just as a lean purchaser will not look for discounts, sales in a lean company will not be allowed to offer them. Product pricing will be based on market pricing and sales will be required to position strategically the company based on quality and capability.

Product

Sales will be given greater latitude in product specifications when dealing with lean clients, being given requirements and a price to design a product to fulfil these requirements, rather than simply being issued blueprints and told to quote for them. Part of this process will involve sales staff working closely with the end client and also internal operations staff to meet customer expectations.

Selling to a lean company will require an ability to rapidly develop new products and shorten the time to market. Lean companies are mistrusting of risky products and dislike prototypes as either are likely to cause production problems for them. Only with finished products, with guaranteed quality, can sales make headway into the lean organisation. Traditional approaches seeking to fill order books before actual production has begun or while products are still in the prototyping stage will not work for lean production.

Sales staff worked with client companies to maximise the ability to carry over existing tooling and processing in their business when new versions of parts or components were released. This could include sales looking at current and future end products and investigating how common parts across a range could be used, for instance, working on using the same part in a luxury vehicle, making a minor modification to make it cost-effective in mid-range vehicles.

The sales group in a lean organisation would also be involved in lifecycle planning, defining the market segments for their products, defining time to market based on their customers' needs and feed this back into production areas. Sales in lean companies have a much greater responsibility in production planning and are as a result expected to have much greater knowledge about both products and production planning.

All the European suppliers struggled with the greater knowledge requirements. Sales teams with no engineering background, no research and development awareness, no knowledge of competitors' products at a technical level and no awareness of operational production processes, were required to retrain rapidly. Sales managers were concerned about how the new way of working would take place – at the time there was (and remains no) model of the transformations that had to take place. Sales teams underwent major training programmes, with significant training support from Nissan and Toyota both individually and in supplier associations. This latter feature involved sales teams coming together with those of previously competing companies to learn together the requirements of lean supply.

Service provision

Any sales group selling to a lean company is expected to offer full service provision, that is, putting together product and service bundles around the parts they offered. This could include selling parts or materials they do not produce or had not previously supplied to ensure the customer is happy. Outside of automotive this has included customising packaging solutions for specific customers, for instance in using shelf-ready packaging or shopping.

After sales service is also a much greater requirement when dealing with lean purchasers. Sales teams are responsible for proactively seeking out any problems with products, logging and investigating these issues, feeding it back into operations for redesign and improvement. Sales staff may actually go out to the production lines of companies and observe production using components they have sold to help develop better products in the future. This has included many sales teams going to Toyota and Nissan to observe production. Despite taking sales teams outside of their comfort zone, many found this an exciting experience and welcomed the opportunity to learn more about how materials were used.

In a lean company the sales teams will also focus more effort on after sales service, seeing this not only as an added-value of the initial sale but as part of the analysis and planning of the product lifecycle. Follow up calls and visits are required to ensure customers are satisfied. In addition, sales teams are expected to hold enough product knowledge that they will know in advance when products or parts will require servicing or replacing – for instance, contacting customers when service intervals are due on a car or mapping out market segments and contacting them when new products are on offer that they may like.

Order management

Order management systems are critically important in selling to and working in a lean company. The stockless nature of just-in-time production practised by lean businesses requires far greater accuracy and forecasting as no buffers are available when mistakes occur. Selling to a lean company will benefit the supplier through smoother and more predictable demand patterns. The closeness between the companies will be supported by much greater information sharing with sales staff. True order amounts required will be transmitted and scheduled over a long period of time. Traditionally distant purchasers can second guess the delivery capability of sales organisations, and over order at one point to ensure stock is available and then not order for periods of time as this is depleted. This can create erratic order patterns that can create difficulty for sales performance targets and also operational fulfilment. In down periods, sales may be faced with offering significant discounts or promotions to other clients, or seeking out new orders, to make up for sales drop offs. The longer planning horizon of the lean company will lead them to demand exact levels of products be delivered at exact times. Supplying to a lean company will involve being asked to supply the exact levels required on a daily and weekly basis, and not minimum order quantities or multiples of them. Ordering in this way helps to eliminate demand amplification through the supply chain (see Forrester, 1961) but will require sales negotiation with operations to meet supply requirements. The first stages towards smooth demand for lean supply in Europe involved putting in two days of safety stock to the purchasing company, to absorb any problems while operational fulfilment improved. This stock was gradually reduced over time until near bufferless production was realised.

Inside a lean company, sales will play roles around the same issues. Sales will be expected to find out true demand levels from customers so that they can help operations better plan production levels over time, without the peaks and troughs caused by erratic order scheduling. Gaining this information from customers, often mistrusting of sales, can be a major problem. Sales plays an important role in winning customer confidence and educating them on the benefits of information sharing.

Sales is expected to help operational planning by checking all orders that come into the company, vetting them to see if unusual items are being ordered or quantities are becoming erratic to assist in production planning. When faced with unusual requirements, sales will be required to work with customers to determine the cause of this and help operational areas of the business plan fulfilment strategies.

Expectations

The sales team will need to work hard to lobby internal departments in the company to change their working practices to meet the different standards of Japanese customers. A lean company will evaluate suppliers on a much wider range of metrics. In addition to the stricter standards on quality, cost and delivery already identified, the broader competence and capability of the company will be assessed. This will include full inspection of company accounts and investment portfolios to ensure the business is solvent and has long run financial stability, thorough examination of the senior management team to asses their competency, assessments of the management structure of the company and its ability to adopt lean working practices. The company will need to adopt certain standards, such as quality certification (usually to ISO 14,000), business continuity planning and metrics of corporate social responsibility (both environmental and relating to workforce management). Many of these issues are beyond the control of the sales department and relate to the core structure of the business. From a traditional role of external selling, there will need to be strategies in place to sell the need to change to other areas of the business.

Faced with customers with such wide requirements, sales teams were overwhelmed with these new requirements. Many felt them to be overly bureaucratic and they failed to see the logic in several of the measures. To demonstrate the value, suppliers were shown their performance on all metrics relative to the supply base and how this was used to support improvement (identifying poor performers and assisting them) so that companies started to equate the measurement systems with improvement rather than punishment or bureaucracy.

Working inside a lean company, sales teams will follow several of these practices. They will be required to provide open book costing to all customers, share information about their management structure, approach and quality standards. They will also practise much greater people specificity than seen in traditional sales. Whereas one liaison may be appointed in key or global account management, even at the consumer level, one sales person would be assigned to a customer for the life of the contract and be expected to work to build a life long relationship.

Education and information

The sales team will play a much greater role in educating their customers and sharing information with them than seen in the traditional adversarial and mistrusting exchanges of western sales practice. As a consequence of this sales will be required to be far more technically knowledgeable about both the product/service they offer and also the processes by which they are produced. This expectation was disconcerting for European sales staff. Many were unprepared for the level of information Japanese companies required. A lot of time was invested by Nissan and Toyota in working with sales and supply teams to educate them on the expectations they held, including hosting visits to Japan to see the standards in practice.

Sales people must demonstrate also command of product trends and competitor products. Sales are expected not only to understand their customers' needs, but the needs of the final consumer. Sales teams were unprepared for the level of information Japanese companies held about their customers and how much they in turn were expected to learn. Sales people must be able to interpret the market conditions of the lean customer and make appropriate adjustments to the product. For instance, in the automotive industry this would include changes to the presentation of vehicle instrumentation, seats, safety systems and how these will shape the product in light of an increasingly ageing population.

Sales people are also expected to know and have made plans to compensate for changes that are happening in the macro-environment. Current trends towards environmentalism are also requiring sales to consider how they can offer better performing products at less cost and environmental degradation. This includes current issues including recycling and take-back laws.

Sales will also be expected to work more closely with other areas of their own business. As the gatekeeper between the company and their customer base they play a critical role in taking information about the customer, which they are expected to maintain in far greater detail than traditional sales, ensuring this is transmitted across the organisation. Sales also plays a policing role ensuring all areas of internal business systems comply with customer ways of working.

The sales team will also pay greater attention to competitors' products and actions. This will include value-engineering and analysis of competitor products at a technical level and potential engagement with direct competitors for collaboration or for business continuity planning.

Inside the lean company, sales will work more closely with customers. This will include more than maintaining contact or visiting clients, extending to taking part in the internal change and improvement activities of customers at the operational level and also at the strategic level playing a role in tracking product lifecycles, replacement planning and more broadly identifying long term markets and growth areas they could supply. As the relationship develops, sales staff may even be seconded into the customer business to work with them on integrated the products they provide with the company.

The changing role of sales: changes inside the department

The changing requirements of selling to a lean company require changes in the internal sales department. The wide ranging demands of customers require much greater investment in education and training of sales personnel so they hold the technical skills required to speak intelligently about products. This will lead to changes to the structure of the department with much greater use of cross-functional teams and employee rotation. Team based working across the company will be the standard. At companies such as Toyota every employee in the company begins in the sales department to educate them on customer requirements. Sales groups will be structured to support the induction and learning of new staff. There will be much more time spent on technical and inter-personal training skills for sales teams to help them work across the business and with their customers. For all staff in the lean company, long term, or in Japan, lifetime employment is standard.

The employment horizon of sales teams also changes, moving towards long term or lifetime employment, rather than continual personnel changes common in western sales departments. Sales teams will also be involved in analysing the efficiency of their own working practices to support the efficiency and continual improvement expected by lean customers. This ensures consistency from the customers' perspective and allows for the sales teams to build up the detailed knowledge about company products and capabilities.

The physical location of the sales team will also change. There may be a centralised sales coordination office but sales staff will be located in production line cells with operational staff to support two-way information exchange and learning. Many of the UK suppliers collocated sales staff into offices alongside production lines. Despite initial concerns about resistance from sales staff, this process was embraced by sales staff who saw it as an opportunity to gain greater responsibility for the teams around them. Part of that responsibility was to support continuous improvement activities at both operational levels and also within the sales group.

For the lean sales team, the key performance indicator will not be sales growth but profitability per customer. This will be supplemented with measures of quality, delivery and cost capabilities of the company. Bonuses will not be paid based on sales (as this leads to discounting or mis-selling to gain business). All sales staff receive a fixed salary and receive a bonus based on the performance of the company as a whole. In the automotive sector this did not have a major unsettling effect due to the stagnant demand in the automotive industry at this time – many welcomed the opportunity for fixed salaries.

The changing role of sales: changes in department–company relationships

Information sharing occurs not only at the customer–sales interface but also at the interfaces between sales and other areas of the company. Sales plays a critical role in understanding customer requirements (such as the very exacting standards on quality and delivery) and then both communicating across the organisation and ensuring these targets are met.

Sales people are expected to be intimately acquainted with the product and production processes they provide. Part of this expectation will be that sales staff and managers take part in job rotations outside of the sales department, into areas such as parts or distribution. Beyond these specific exchanges sales is expected to be closely integrated with other areas of the business – only then can they provide the detail of information the lean customer provides. The sales teams selling to a lean company may spend a third to a half of their time working on cross-functional teams inside their own organisation, helping them understand their own products and processes and also passing customer information back into operational areas of the business. Job rotation into operational areas and use of cross-functional project teams will be key parts of sales activity. While this takes sales staff away from the task of selling, it enables them to sell better, by understanding organisational capability better. Product knowledge is expected to be at the same level as production or operational engineers and not simply to sales-brochure standards.

Sales time spent with internal groups also ensures that organisational capabilities continue to be shaped based on a detailed understanding of customer requirements as sales take part in designing operational fulfilment. For instance, sales teams in Toyota played a key role in redesigning the Aygo small-car as consumers highlighted design issues that failed to meet requirements, such as an electronic window only on the driver's side.

Discussion

The movements towards lean production and organisation across the economy are shaping a new role for the modern sales team. In this paper we have examined some of the key challenges. The changes faced require a shift in sales strategy towards a collaborative and open approach to working with customers, openness and information sharing across organisational boundaries, and a different way of working inside the organisation. Instead of competing based on price, sales competes on the capability of the organisation and plays a key role in shaping that capability. A detailed understanding of the customer is captured by sales teams who may spend up to half of their time working with departments inside their own company to share this intelligence to design better products and processes that meet customer requirements. A culture of customer-led business is also present, through the establishment of mechanisms and processes that focus the entire company on the end customer, through cross-functional working, job rotation. The culmination of these activities could be argued to change the basic strategic purpose of the sales group away from being a sales-force towards being a marketing-force.

The divergence of sales from marketing activity is a common theme in the marketing literature. Early academics highlighted marketing as fundamentally different to sales (Kolter & Levy, 1969). Key differences between marketing and sales include: sales focus on sales volume, not profits or profit planning, sales focus on the short run, sales does not conduct market analysis, planning and control while marketing does (Kotler, 1977). Under marketing, rather than seeking to sell products to customers based on what the company produced (through price promotion or advertising), the company would seek to understand what the customer actually wanted and produce this (Greyser, 1998; Keener, 1960; Keith, 1960). Marketing is about understanding what the market values so this value can be offered to it by the company (Kotler, 1972).

Mechanisms to realise these marketing concepts in practice have focused on market orientation. This has been differentially defined around: cultural issues where marketing is about creating a company-wide culture focused on the creation of superior values for customers (Narver & Slater, 1990; Slater & Narver, 1994); focused on market intelligence – describing organisation-wide generation of market intelligence about current and future customer needs that is then disseminated across the company and used to design the organisation's value creation systems (Jaworski & Kohli, 1993; Kohli & Jaworski, 1990; Kohli, Jaworski, & Kumar, 1993); or customer centred – a set of beliefs that put the customers' interests first and incorporate the needs of other stakeholders in the business (including management and employees) (Desphande, Farley, & Webster, 1993, 1997). Bringing these themes together Deshpande and Farley (1996, 1998) describe marketing orientation as 'the set of cross functional processes and activities directed at creating and satisfying customers through continuous need assessment' (1996, p. 14). Researchers have emphasised the cross-functional aspects of marketing orientation, noting that these activities are no longer the sole responsibility of marketing (or sales) departments, but of everyone in the organisation (Deshpande, 2002; Greyser, 1998; Webster, 1992). Key themes highlight marketing activity as based on holding a fundamental understanding of the customer, sharing this understanding across the entire business into other functional areas and shaping the design of the operational fulfillment systems of the business. Despite academic acknowledgement of the importance of organisational-wide marketing awareness, for most organisations, sales-push rather than building any real understanding of customers' needs, requirements and fulfilling them, remains the dominant approach (Kotler, 1977; Piercy, 2008). Despite the clear message that only with a marketing focus, across all areas of the business, can the long term profitability of the company be assured (Kotler, 1972, 1977) most marketing departments in practice continue to conduct sales based activity (Day, 1994; Denison & McDonald, 1995; Hult, Cravens, & Sheth, 2001; Webster, 1998). The academic marketing community has done little to respond to this situation or to shape a better role for sales strategy, linking this back to customer requirements and demands (Brown, 1994; Day, 1998; Deshpande, 1999; McDonald & Wilson, 2002).

In tracing the changes in sales created by the operational forces of lean production, sales activity is shifting towards a marketing-orientated strategy, organisation and approach to the customer (see Figure 2). The changing requirements placed on the sales team by lean production include: much greater time spent on intelligence generation of their customers and end consumers; cultural changes in the setup of the sales department with greater cross-functional working; establishing long run partnerships with customers; significant time spent working with operational areas of the business to disseminate customer knowledge; using this knowledge to shift the company towards producing products on the customers' terms and not their own. No longer are the sales team taking established products or cost systems out and hard-selling, they are being required to serve the inherent needs and wants of their customers. For European and American companies this may be involuntary and dictated to them as a requirement of gaining business with a lean company, but the changing strategy, perspective and actions that take place are real. The basis of sales activity is being redirected away from sales-push towards the classical definitions of the marketing concept and marketing organisation – understanding customer needs, sharing this intelligence across functional boundaries and designing products and services to meet customer requirements. The changes taking place inside the organisation may be uncomfortable and disconcerting for the sales managers, but the changes in all the case companies examined have benefitted the long term survival and profitability of the organisation as they have established long run, mutually beneficial relationships with their customers.

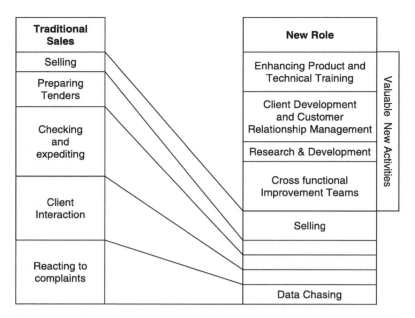

Figure 2.   From sales-force to marketing-force.

Conclusion

The rise of the lean operational form cannot be ignored. The spread of lean concepts from automotive into all sectors of the economy continues to accelerate. The buyer–supplier relationships of the lean organisation stand apart to those seen in traditional purchasing relationships. Despite interest in collaborative or partnership sourcing in the supply chain field, work in this area has never investigated the changing roles and requirements of the sales team. Work on lean operations has looked at the production capabilities of suppliers and how these change, but has ignored the role of sales people as those responsible for leading the change inside the company. The sales management literature to date has also omitted any consideration of how the sales teams' structure and strategy is altered under lean sourcing.

Key changes identified in this paper include: moves towards long term relationships between sales and purchasers; the end of price based sales and a shift towards competing based on organisational capability; the end of sales-volume based bonuses and the introduction of fixed salary schemes and bonus incentives based on company performance as a whole; the requirements that sales staff hold much greater knowledge about the products they sell and the methods by which these are produced; the reshaping of the sales department with cross-functional working and staff taken outside of the sales department and onto the production line; and, the moves towards long term and lifetime employment of sales staff.

There are significant challenges in transitioning a workforce with typically short employment horizons (with a resultant lack of in-depth product or market knowledge), driven by bonus-based selling, towards a lean based marketing-force. There requires a fundamental shift in the strategic organising logic of the sales department. This will involve a movement away from a functional silo to a strategic process owned by the whole business, shifting the contract of employment and principles underpinning it, movement away from thinking of sales as overhead to more of a direct responsibility and significant investment in training and support for sales staff. The benefits on offer for the company are based on the formation of long run partnership agreements with growth businesses. For the sales department, activity becomes more interesting and less chaotic, helping sales staff realise their true potential, giving them a better role to play and professionalising sales as an activity.

There were difficulties in these changes in all case companies. In the automotive sector examined, bonuses were so depressed abandoning them was not problematic, in other sectors where bonuses may contribute significant amounts of take home pay, this could be more problematic, although many companies are already moving to company based incentives. Many sales teams were unprepared for the level of knowledge required, the depth of training that had to be completed, were sceptical about being relocated onto production lines and dealing with what they saw as the bureaucratic requirements of customers. The biggest problem for the sales groups in this paper was a lack of awareness of what the real requirements and issues involved in selling to Japanese companies were. For these companies, focal lean organisations like Toyota and Nissan invested time and effort in educating suppliers, training and supporting sales teams. In other markets, large and often oligopolistic customers may not be so generous and sales strategy needs to lead the way in changing the philosophy and approach of sales management. In this paper we have outlined the major challenges to assist in this process.

Greater research is still needed to examine the role of the sales and marketing personnel in the face of lean operational changes. From our initial findings we have proposed that a shift in strategic organisation occurs with the sales-force becoming a marketing-force, conducting the activities traditionally associated with the marketing concept or orientation. This can only be beneficial for the company.

References

Altshuler, A., Anderson, M., Jones, D., Roos, D., & Womack, J. (1986). *The future of the automobile*. Boston, MA: MIT Press.

Anderson Consulting. (1992). *Lean enterprise benchmarking report*. London: Anderson Consulting.

Anderson Consulting. (1994). *Global lean enterprise benchmarking report*. London: Anderson Consulting.

Balle, F., & Balle, M. (2005). *The goldmine: A novel of lean turnaround*. Boston, MA: Lean Enterprise Institute.

Brown, S. (1994). Marketing as multiplex: Screening postmodernism. *European Journal of Marketing*, 28(8/9), 27–51.

Chandra, C., & Kumar, S. (2000). Supply chain management in theory and practice. *Industrial Management and Data Systems*, 100(3), 100–114.

Chopra, S., Lovejoy, W., & Yano, C. (2004). Five decades of operations management and the prospects ahead. *Management Science*, 50(1), 8–14.

Cox, A., Lonsdale, C., Sanderson, J., & Watson, G. (2004). *Business relationships for competitive advantage: Managing alignment and misalignment in buyer and supplier transactions*. Basingstoke: Palgrave Macmillan.

Day, G. (1994). The capabilities of market-driven organizations. *Journal of Marketing*, 58(4), 37–52.

Day, G. (1998). Aligning the organisation to the market. In D. Lehmann & K. Jocz (Eds.), *Reflections on the futures of marketing* (pp. 67–96). Cambridge, MA: Marketing Science Institute.

Deming, W.E. (1982a). *Out of crisis*. Cambridge: Cambridge University Press.

Deming, W.E. (1982b). *Quality, production and competitive position*. Boston, MA: MIT Centre for Advanced Engineering Study.

Denison, T., & McDonald, M. (1995). The role of marketing, past, present and future. *Journal of Marketing Practice*, 1(1), 54–76.

Deshpande, R. (1999). Foreseeing marketing. *Journal of Marketing*, 63(Special Issue), 164–167.

Deshpande, R. (2002). Performance companies. *International Journal of Medical Marketing*, 2(3), 225–231.

Deshpande, R., & Farley, J. (1996). Understanding market orientation: A prospectively designed meta-analysis of three market orientation scales. Marketing Science Institute Working Paper Report 96–125.

Deshpande, R., & Farley, J. (1998). Measuring market orientation: Generalization and synthesis. *Journal of Market Focused Management*, 2(3), 213–232.

Deshpande, R., Farley, J., & Webster, F. (1993). Corporate culture, customer orientation, and innovativeness in Japanese firms: A quadrad analysis. *Journal of Marketing*, 57(January), 23–37.

Deshpande, R., Farley, J., & Webster, F. (1997). Factors affecting organizational performance: A five country comparison. Marketing Science Institute Working Paper Report 97–108.

Dyer, J. (1997). Effective interfirm collaboration: How firms minimise transaction costs and maximise transaction value. *Strategic Management Journal*, 18(7), 535–556.

EEF. (2007). *High value: How UK manufacturing has changed*. London: The Manufacturers Association.

Egan, J. (1998). *Rethinking construction: The Egan report*. London: Construction Task Force.

Forrester, J. (1961). *Industrial dynamics*. Portland, OR: Productivity Press.

Fujimoto, T. (1999). *The evolution of a manufacturing system at Toyota*. Oxford: Oxford University Press.

Greyser, S. (1998). Janus and marketing. In D. Lehmann & K. Jocz (Eds.), *Reflections on the futures of marketing* (pp. 3–14). Cambridge, MA: Marketing Science Institute.

Hayes, R.H., & Wheelwright, S.C. (1984). *Restoring our competitive edge: Competing through manufacturing*. New York: Wiley.

Helper, S. (1991). How much has really changed between US automakers and their suppliers? *Sloan Management Review*, 32(4), 15–29.

Hines, P. (1994). *Creating world class suppliers*. London: Pitman.

Hult, G., Cravens, D., & Sheth, J. (2001). Competitive advantage in the global marketplace. *Journal of Business Research*, 51(1), 1–3.

Jaworski, B., & Kohli, A. (1993). Market orientation: Antecedents and consequences. *Journal of Marketing*, 57(July), 53–70.

Jones, D. (2001). Tesco.com: Delivering home shopping. *ECR Journal*, 1(1), 37–43.

Jones, D., & Mitchell, A. (2006). *Lean thinking for the NHS*. London: NHS Confederation Report.

Keener, J. (1960). Marketing's job for the 1960s. *Journal of Marketing*, 24(3), 1–6.

Keith, R. (1960). The marketing revolution. *Journal of Marketing*, 24(3), 35–38.

Kohli, A., & Jaworski, B. (1990). Market orientation: The construct, research propositions and managerial implications. *Journal of Marketing*, 54(April), 1–18.

Kohli, A., Jaworski, B., & Kumar, A. (1993). MARKOR: A measure of market orientation. *Journal of Marketing Research*, 30(November), 467–477.

Kotler, P. (1972). A generic concept of marketing. *Journal of Marketing*, 35(April), 46–54.

Kotler, P. (1977). From sales obsession to marketing effectiveness. *Harvard Business Review*, 55(6), 67–76.

Kotler, P., & Levy, S. (1969). Broadening the concept of marketing. *Journal of Marketing*, 33(January), 10–15.

Kurogane, K. (1993). *Cross functional management: Principles*. Portland, OR: Productivity Press.

Lamming, R. (1996). Squaring lean supply with supply chain management. *International Journal of Operations and Production Management*, 16(2), 183–196.

Liker, J. (2003). *The Toyota way*. New York: McGrawHill.

Liker, J., & Hoseus, M. (2007). *Toyota culture: The heart and soul of the Toyota way*. New York: McGrawHill.

Lummus, R., & Vokurka, R. (1999). Defining supply chain management: A historical perspective and practical guidelines. *Industrial Management and Data System*, 99(1), 11–17.

MacBeth, D., & Ferguson, N. (1994). *Partnership sourcing*. London: Pitman Publishing.

McDonald, M., & Wilson, H. (2002). *The new marketing*. Oxford: Butterworth Heinemann.

Merli, G. (1991). *Co-makership: The new supply strategy for manufacturers*. Portland, OR: Productivity Press.

Monden, Y. (1983). *The Toyota production system*. Portland, OR: Productivity Press.

Monden, Y. (1997). *The Toyota management system*. Portland, OR: Productivity Press.

Monden, Y. (1998). *Toyota production system: An integrated approach to just-in-time*. New York: Engineering and Management.

Narver, J., & Slater, S. (1990). The effect of a market orientation on business profitability. *Journal of Marketing, 20*(October), 20–35.

Nishiguchi, T. (1994). *Strategic industrial sourcing*. Oxford: Oxford University Press.

Ohno, T. (1988). *The Toyota production system: Beyond large-scale production*. Portland, OR: Productivity Press.

Piercy, N.F. (2008). *Market-led strategic change*. Oxford: Butterworth-Heinemann.

Piercy, N.F., & Morgan, N. (1997). The impact of lean thinking and the lean enterprise on marketing: Threat or synergy. *Journal of Marketing Management, 13*(7), 679–693.

Rowley, I. (2008, October 20). How Toyota plans to beat the downturn. *Business Week*. Retrieved January 20, 2009, from http://www.businessweek.com

Sako, M. (1992). *Price, quality and trust: Inter-firm relations in Britain and Japan*. Cambridge: Cambridge Press.

Schonberger, R. (1986). *World class manufacturing: The lessons of simplicity applied*. New York: Free Press.

Shaw, T., Lengyel, A., & Ferre, G. (2004). *An assessment of the degree of implementation of the lean aerospace initiative principles and practices within the US aerospace and defense industry*. Virginia: Government Electronics and Information Technology Association.

Shingo, S. (1981). *Study of the Toyota production systems*. Tokyo: Japan Management Association.

Shingo, S. (1988). *Non-stock production: The Shingo system for continuous improvement*. Cambridge: Productivity Press.

Slater, S., & Narver, J. (1994). Does competitive environment moderate the market orientation–performance relationship? *Journal of Marketing, 58*(January), 46–55.

Smitka, M. (1991). *Competitive ties*. Columbia: Columbia University Press.

Suzaki, K. (1987). *New manufacturing challenge: Techniques for continuous improvement*. New York: Free Press.

Toyota. (1997). *Supplier's guide for doing business with Toyota*. Nagoya, Japan: Toyota Motor Corporation.

Toyota. (1998). *Toyota logistics manual*. Nagoya, Japan: Toyota Motor Corporation.

Toyota. (2008). *Toyota annual accounts*. Nagoya, Japan: Toyota Motor Corporation.

Toyota. (2009). *Toyota supplier policy*. Toyota Motor Corporation, Nagoya, Japan. Retrieved January 20, 2009, from www.toyotasupplier.com

Webster, F. (1992). The changing role of marketing in the corporation. *Journal of Marketing, 56*(4), 1–17.

Webster, F. (1998). The future role of marketing in the organization. In D. Lehmann & K. Jocz (Eds.), *Reflections on the futures of marketing* (pp. 39–66). Cambridge, MA: Marketing Science Institute.

Wincell, J. (2003). *Lean supply chain management: A handbook for strategic procurement*. Portland, OR: Productivity Press.

Womack, J., & Jones, D. (1996). *Lean thinking*. London: Touchstone.

Womack, J., & Jones, D. (2003). *Lean thinking* (2nd ed.). London: Free Press.

Womack, J., Jones, D., & Roos, D. (1990). *The machine that changed the world*. New York: Rawson Associates.

An enterprise-wide strategic stakeholder approach to sales ethics

Linda Ferrell and O.C. Ferrell

Department of Marketing, University of New Mexico, Albuquerque, NM 87131, USA

A framework for an enterprise-wide strategic stakeholder approach to sales ethics is developed to address ethical sales performance. Stakeholder orientation goes beyond market orientation and customer orientation and provides the foundation for an organizational ethical culture and an ethical sales subculture. Organizational values and norms can dictate modes of behavior and help balance stakeholder interests. Understanding organizational ethical decision making helps to identify risk and aids in the development of appropriate programs to prevent misconduct. A strategic focus includes an ethical organizational culture, guidelines and boundaries for conduct, as well as continuous improvement.

Overview

There is evidence that strategic sales leadership, which builds on an ethical organizational culture, and a sales management control strategy contributes to ethical decisions in business to business (B2B) sales (Ingram, LaForge, & Schwepker, 2007). The sales force plays a pivotal role in developing transparency and trust with stakeholders. Market orientation with a sales customer orientation could be the first step in developing a concern for all stakeholders. A positive association has been found between stakeholder orientation (SO), market and financial performance, reputation, and employee commitment (Maignan, Hult, Ferrell, & Gonzalez, 2009). An ethical organization develops a strategic perspective and recognizes the interface with relevant stakeholders, and develops principled performance and an ethical culture.

The purpose of this paper is to provide a framework for a strategic approach to an enterprise-wide stakeholder perspective that encompasses sales ethics. An ethical sales function in an organization should not operate as a silo independent from the organizational culture as a whole. The management of ethical risks that are specific to an industry or firm, as well as ethical risks in the sales function, must be managed. To fulfill its obligations, the sales force must consider very specific risks associated with interactions with customers and communications about products and organizational competence. Ignoring stakeholders can create reputational, and even legal, issues. The salesperson can either build long-term trust or destroy it and the reputation of a firm in minutes.

Our approach in this analysis is first to use a stakeholder framework to position the sales function in a strategic role to participate in the development and implementation of ethical marketing practice. While stakeholder orientation is an organizational philosophy, customer orientation is consistent with an ethical sales force. A strategic approach to ethics develops a process for addressing stakeholder issues and concerns including: (1) creating a strategic focus on stakeholders, risk tolerance and culture; (2) developing guidelines and boundaries for acceptable practices; and (3) creating mechanisms for continuous improvement. We address the nature of organizational ethical decision making and the role of enterprise-wide risk assessment and a principled approach to establishing boundaries for ethical decisions.

Foundations of a strategic approach to sales ethics: stakeholder orientation

Stakeholder orientation (Freeman, 1984) considers the interests of all individuals and groups to whom the business is responsible. The three conditions that help identify stakeholders interests are: (1) the groups or individuals can be positively or negatively impacted by organizational activities and/or are concerned about the impact of organizational decisions and actions on other groups; (2) the individuals or group can grant or deny resources to the organization; and (3) the individuals or group valued by the organizational culture (Frooman, 1999; Maignan & Ferrell, 2004; Rowley, 1997). The stakeholder framework rests on the normative foundation that 'all persons or groups with legitimate interests participating in an enterprise do so to obtain benefits and that there is no prima facie priority of one set of interests and benefits over another' (Mitchell, Agle, & Wood, 1997, p. 868).

While the stakeholder perspective recognizes the intrinsic value of all stakeholders, sales strategies based on a market orientation (MO) have focused on customers and competitors more than other stakeholders (Day, 1994; Narver & Slater, 1990). Studies show that sales orientation (focused on getting the sale) based on customer orientation (focused on enhancing customer value) is a key forecaster of salesperson job performance. High performance occurs when salespeople focus their energy on identifying the customer's individual needs and offer products to satisfy those needs (Jaramillo, Ladik, Marshall, & Mulki, 2007). On the other hand, MO is an enterprise-wide concept. One study found a weak link between MO norms and customer orientation of the salesperson (Farrell, 2005). This signals a need for better implementation of MO norms to sales force behavior. Elevating one group of stakeholder's interests over all other interests can have a significant impact on employee behavior, as evidenced by Wal-Mart's earlier focus on 'saving customers' money' at the expense of employee, supplier, community, and governmental and regulatory groups' interests. Employees, customers, shareholders, regulators, and suppliers are key stakeholders. Competitors, a key concern in MO, can be considered a secondary stakeholder and are important to an organization because their actions have the power to influence the outcomes of marketing strategies.

Stakeholder orientation as a component of sales strategy

The stakeholder perspective has been a pervasive part of the marketing literature on ethics and social responsibility (Blodgett, Lu, Rose, & Vitell, 2001; Maignan & Ferrell, 2004; Sen, Bhattacharya, & Korschun, 2006). The utilization of the stakeholder concept in marketing appears to be a relevant tactic, and using such an approach can be helpful in strategizing about addressing stakeholder needs, interests, and demands (Bhattacharya & Korschun, 2008; Polonsky, 1996). While MO considers the importance of factors other than customers, it does not appear to have as broad a construct as SO in addressing relevant interests (Deshpandé, Farley, & Webster, 1993).

We propose the use of SO to better manage the sales function in a strategic framework. SO embraces both organizational and sales behaviors that encourage all participants to continuously be aware of, and act positively upon, stakeholders' current and emerging interests. SO makes organizational participants actively engage to address the concerns and needs of relevant stakeholders. The first step in understanding ethical issues is recognizing stakeholder interests and concerns. Stakeholders are individuals, groups, even communities, that can directly or indirectly affect a firm's activities. Although most corporations have emphasized shareholders as the most important stakeholder group, the failure to consider all significant stakeholders can lead to ethical lapses. In sales organizations, stakeholders include employees, customers, suppliers, investors, regulators, communities, as well as shareholders. Some executives believe that if their companies adopt a MO and focus only on customers and competitors, all other groups will be adequately supported. Sales must include a strong customer orientation to be successful, but, failure to recognize the needs and potential impact of employees, suppliers, regulators, special-interest groups, communities, and the media, can lead to adverse consequences. For example, investment advisors from the Swiss bank UBS helped many wealthy Americans hide assets and avoid paying taxes in the USA (Barrett & Novak, 2009). In theory, this was the implementation of customer orientation. This scheme damaged all stakeholders and tarnished the ethical reputation of UBS. Consequences from ignoring stakeholder groups can be especially dire in the sales organization, where the boundary-spanning role of sales allows for significant communication outreach with customers, suppliers, communities, as well as others.

Therefore, the sales organization needs to consider enterprise-wide stakeholders and to identify and prioritize their concerns about organizational activities, and gather information to respond to significant individuals, groups, and communities. These groups apply their own values and standards to their perception of many diverse issues. They supply resources (e.g. capital, labor, expertise, infrastructure, sales, etc.) that are more-or-less critical to a firm's long-term survival, and their ability to withdraw (or threaten to withdraw). In essence, these resources give them power. The B2B sales function has a special responsibility because of the sales and service they provide and the need to develop trust in providing deliverables. Most salespeople operate with significant autonomy in their sales role. Maintaining standards for behavior in consideration of diverse stakeholders is essential to long-term success. The specific role context of the sales force sometimes is limited to maintaining and increasing sales. The sales area has to utilize an organizational and cross-functional perspective. Strategic oversight is required to maintain a more holistic focus on stakeholder issues.

One approach to stakeholders is to deal proactively with their concerns and ethical issues and to stimulate a sense of bonding with the firm. When an organization listens to stakeholder concerns and tries to resolve issues, the result is tangible benefits that can translate into customer loyalty, employee commitment, supplier partnerships, and improved corporate reputation. Achieving this requires going beyond industry standards and basic regulatory requirements by genuinely listening to stakeholders and addressing their concerns. In the sales organization, transparency and truthfulness about products is a necessity. There is a requirement that top management or the board of directors exercise due diligence in managing their sales goals. When firms focus exclusively on profits and financial incentives for employees to perform, they can lose sight of risks and potential ethical and legal issues. For example, the European Commission levied a €676 million fine against the wax industry for creating a cartel that constituted an anti-trust violation. Sales executives had meetings in hotels across Europe to fix prices. The so-called 'paraffin mafia' included firms such as South Africa's Sasol, France's Total, and the USA's Exxon Mobil (*Ethisphere*, 2008). To achieve results, employees may be permitted to bend rules if it benefits their performance. The problem can worsen if the firm limits transparency of sales executives' activities, and an ethical disaster such as antitrust violations may occur.

Stakeholder values and norms' role in responsible behavior

Marketers have historically tended to engage in socially responsible behaviors only in the presence of stakeholder power and influence. Social and regulatory groups are increasingly pressuring business to operate more responsibly and much of what is happening is being driven from outside influence, not proactive behavior. Marketers, therefore, limit their responsibility initiatives to those issues of concern to the most powerful and visible stakeholder communities. This view has some merit, especially since managers and employees form stakeholder communities that actively defend specific norms and values within the firm. However, organizations may be driven to commit to a specific cause independently of any stakeholder pressure. Businesses may also want to exceed stakeholder expectations. For example, BP Global deals openly and transparently with shareholders as well as other stakeholders. Their goal is to set appropriate external targets in line with its internal targets and report against them periodically. The group also acts in accordance with the principles of the Extractive Industries Transparency Initiative (BP, 2009).

Thus, organizational values and norms can dictate modes of behavior that are more stringent than those demanded by various stakeholder communities (Maignan & Ferrell, 2004). Organizations such as Medtronics have senior managers attend medical surgeries to better understand the use, benefits, and gain direct feedback on how their products work in these critical situations. Cisco believes that selling a product without extensive after sales service to the account is irresponsible selling.

Clear organizational values and norms are also needed to select among conflicting stakeholder demands. A certain sales organization could indeed be faced with equally powerful stakeholders whose views of social responsibility imply different business practices. For example, while customers may demand environmentally friendly products, shareholders may question green investments because of their high costs and uncertain returns. Accordingly, organizational values and norms are especially useful to guide socially responsible practices when they specify the nature of either relevant stakeholder communities or important stakeholder issues. For example, the pharmaceutical company Bristol-Myers Squibb states on its website: 'Our company's core values ... center on sustaining and improving the lives of people throughout the world. This specifically includes our employees and shareholders, customers and consumers, suppliers and contractors, and members of the communities in which we operate.' Noticeably, even though strong organizational values and norms are important, they are not sufficient to ensure responsible corporate behaviors: they may fail to account for the evolving norms and issues valued by powerful stakeholder communities. Therefore, businesses must be capable of defining their values and norms while concurrently keeping abreast of those of their stakeholders. Values and norms are key factors in determining socially responsible and ethical behaviors.

Organizational ethical culture and sales ethical subculture

Although individuals must make ethical choices, they often do so in committees, group meetings, and through discussion with colleagues. In the sales organization, team selling increasingly is used to deal with complex products and solutions to business challenges, however, the lack of individual accountability and cross-functional teams can result in uneven understandings of acceptable and unacceptable behavior. Ethical decisions in the workplace are guided by the organization's culture and the influence of coworkers, superiors, and subordinates. A significant element of organizational culture is a firm's ethical climate – its character or conscience. Whereas a firm's overall culture establishes values that guide a wide range of behaviors for members of the organization, its ethical climate focuses specifically on issues of right and wrong. Codes of conduct and ethics policies, top management's and coworker's actions on ethical issues, and the opportunity for misconduct all contribute to an organization's ethical climate. In fact, the ethical climate determines whether certain dilemmas are perceived as having a level of ethical intensity that requires a decision. In providing financial incentives for performance, salespeople may only see the rewards for the sale, not the risks or consequences of unethical behavior.

The sales function can have a unique ethical climate or subculture within the ethical culture of the organization. Therefore, the sales ethical subculture influences managers and coworkers and may create conditions that either limit or permit misconduct. If these conditions act to provide rewards – such as financial gain, recognition, promotion, or simply the good feeling from a job well done – for unethical conduct, the opportunity for further unethical conduct may exist. For example, a company policy that does not provide for punishment of employees who violate a rule (e.g. not to misrepresent competitors' products or competence) effectively creates an opportunity for that behavior because it allows individuals to break the rule without fear of consequences. Thus, organizational policies, processes, and other factors may contribute to the opportunity to act unethically.

Such opportunities often relate to salesperson's immediate job context – where they work, with whom they work, and the nature of the work. The specific work situation includes the motivational 'carrots and sticks' that managers can use to influence employee behavior. Pay raises, bonuses, and public recognition are carrots, or positive reinforcement, whereas reprimands, pay penalties, demotions, and even firings act as sticks, or negative reinforcement. For example, a sales manager that is publicly recognized and given a large bonus for operating a successful regional sales force while knowingly condoning unethical tactics in the field will probably be motivated to use unethical sales tactics in the future, even if such behavior goes against his or her personal value system.

Performance outcomes have a significant impact on how sales managers deal with employees. Average and poor performers are generally disciplined and managed more according to the rules and culture of the organization whereas top performers are able to 'bend the rules' and engage in behaviors that would not be tolerated at lower performance thresholds (Bellizzi & Bristol, 2005; Bellizzi & Hasty, 2003). Sales managers and key account managers have an incredible impact on quarterly earnings. Even heavily regulated insurance companies and investment banks developed corporate cultures that provided incentives for selling high risk products. Merrill Lynch, as well investment banks such as Goldman Sachs, Lehman Brothers, and Bear Stearns ratified incentives, bonuses, and compensation packages based on sales, not ethics, transparency, or stakeholder concerns. All of these firms contributed to a global financial collapse because of the influence of their corporate culture on their sales subculture, which encouraged reckless speculation that ignored the interests of shareholders, customers, and regulatory agencies. Enron gave account managers and traders a bonus system to inflate future profitability before outcomes of sales transactions were known. The incentives in these companies for misconduct were systematic and cultural, not merely rogue sales managers.

Ethical decision making in sales

A strategic approach to managing sales ethics starts with an understanding of how ethical decisions are made in the context of an organization. Research indicates that both individual and organizational factors influence ethical decision making (McClaren, 2000). Individual factors include age, education, individual values, job tenure, and other personal factors. For example, women tend to be more ethical than men in the workplace. Individuals who have longer tenure on the job and more education also tend to make more ethical decisions (Loe, Ferrell, & Mansfield, 2000).

Jaramillo et al. (2007) found that 'lone wolf' tendencies in salespeople lower contextual performance as represented by helping, courtesy, and sportsmanship. Personal ethical perspectives related to teleological and deontological philosophies have been found to influence individual ethical decisions (Hunt & Vitell, 1986). Deontology focuses on the principles, rights, or duties, rather than the consequences of an action. Teleology, on the other hand, focuses on the final results, or the consequences, of an act. Utilitarianism is a teleological philosophy that is concerned with achieving the greatest good for the greatest number of people. Cognitive moral development is a personal factor that indicates moral maturity but it is difficult to measure and connect to organizational ethical decision making (Robin, Gordon, Jordan, & Reidenback, 1996).

Organizational culture, the subculture or ethical climate of the sales force and the sales role and environment are areas for strategic management (Ferrell, Johnston, & Ferrell, 2007). The foundation for identifying ethical issues is a SO that listens to stakeholder issues, evaluates risks, and responds with guidelines for behavior. An organizational culture provides values and norms for the entire enterprise and the sales organization subculture should be based on a purposeful plan, commitment, and effective leadership for day-to-day implementation. Unless top managers understand how ethical decision making occurs in the context of their specific organization and functional area, then they will not be able to identify ethical risk and develop appropriate programs to prevent misconduct.

Ethical decision-making models in marketing, by Dubinsky and Loken (1989), Ferrell and Gresham (1985), Ferrell, Gresham, and Fraedrich (1989), Hunt and Vitell (2006), and Wotruba (1990) help define an understanding of how ethical decisions are made in a sales context. These models have provided a conceptual framework for sales ethics research that reinforces our understanding and provides strategic insights and direction for managers (Ferrell et al., 2007). Research indicates that members of the sales organization do not differ from members of other marketing professions with respect to personal moral perspectives, or perceptions of ethical problems and feasible resolution (Singhapakdi & Vitell, 1992). While Ferrell and Gresham (1985) proposed that attitudes will affect ethical decision making, Dubinsky and Loken (1989) suggested that these attitudes are affected by behavioral and normative beliefs. In an effort to extend sales ethics research, Wotruba (1990) developed the EDAP (Ethical Decision Action Process) sales ethical framework that included four major elements: (1) the moral decision structure; (2) characteristics of the decision maker; (3) situational moderators; and (4) outcomes. This framework enabled researchers to direct research activity to specific components of the sales ethical decision process.

Opportunity relates to sales managers' immediate job context, where they work, with whom they work and the nature of that work. In addition, the immediate job context includes motivational tactics (carrots and sticks) that managers use to influence behavior (Ferrell, Fraedrich, & Ferrell, 2008). Increasing sales and managing the sales force is a pressured environment for performance. It is easier for individuals under pressure to perform, to engage in behaviors that are unethical and potentially illegal (Piercy & Lane, 2007). From an individual perspective, examining an account manager or sales managers' moral philosophy of deontology (rules and principles over negative consequences) should help understand deep seated cognitive processes for making decisions. Hunt and Vitell (1986) state that these entrenched philosophies of decision making are translated into action through the mediating variable of intentions. From a teleology perspective, the process of making an ethical decision will involve evaluating the consequences to relevant stakeholder groups.

Those sales managers who embrace egoism, which means focusing one's own self-interest, a central concern of teleological thinking, have the potential to be rogue decision makers that ignore the sales subculture of formal ethics and engage in misconduct to benefit themselves. In a positive finding, Cohen and Reed (2006) discovered that the organizational culture will be the major influence of ethical decision making because organizational members rely on context-specific attitudes. Once attitudes are recalled for evaluating an ethical decision, a perceived readiness will prompt actual behavior. If the conclusion is that a situation raises ethical issues, then the situation should provoke a recollection of past instances of ethical decision making to determine a decision. This means that strategic leadership that creates a positive sales ethics subculture and effective compliance standards can control rogue employees' behavior. Individuals working in a culture that is transparent creates accountability through internal controls that have the potential to develop appropriate context-specific attitudes and behaviors.

The challenges of managing risk

For most sales organizations, there is a fear of discovering illegal activity or misconduct. Given its position within the organization, the sales staff often finds itself on the front line of serious ethical and legal misconduct. Sales staff can find opportunities for price-fixing, bribery, misrepresentation of product quality, conflicts of interest, channel stuffing, and facilitation of accounting fraud; as well as human resource issues related to discrimination, sexual harassment, and abusive behavior toward coworkers. All of these potential issues should be considered threats that must be monitored and managed. Sales organizations need to identify potential risks and to uncover activities that, if left undetected, could devastate the sales function, not to mention the organization as a whole. Therefore, organizations should have a plan and infrastructure in place to help determine risks and to deal with them as quickly as possible. Organizations should never seek to cover up, ignore, or assume that no one will discover ethical and legal lapses. They instead must seek to discover, expose, and resolve issues as soon as they occur. All sales organizations occasionally have problems with misconduct, and dealing with these events is the only effective way to manage relationships with stakeholders and retain the organization's reputation. The existence of plaintiff-friendly civil litigation can destroy a company's reputation and draw intense scrutiny (Brewer, Chandler, & Ferrell, 2006).

For most sales executives, this potential of discovering serious misconduct or illegal activity somewhere in the organization is their greatest fear. They worry that if misconduct is made public, it could be used by various stakeholders, including secondary stakeholders such as the mass media and competitors, to undermine the firm's reputation. Managers worry that they will discover an ethical situation that is beyond their control which could jeopardize their careers, or their organizations. Fear is such a paralyzing emotion that the temptation to cover up, ignore, or become complacent rather than taking a proactive stance regarding misconduct, can become a daily survival method. Consider this conversation overheard by one of the co-authors. A sales manager told a salesperson to stop talking when he attempted to broach the need to pay a bribe to secure a key account. The sales manager told the sales rep, 'Your job is to get the business any way you can. I don't want to know the details.' This conversation is a common scenario in many sales managers' offices.

In general, the legal system focuses on individual misconduct, rather than organizational systems and ethical culture failures. The case of Bernard Madoff, LLC and accusations that Madoff operated history's largest known Ponzi scheme were made evident to the US Securities and Exchange Commission (SEC) on many occasions over a number of years. However, the SEC was unable to uncover and identify the complex network of feeder funds, and individual agents that were allegedly selling their clients Madoff's investment services. The Madoff Ponzi scheme was sold to the most respected banks, insurance companies, and hedge funds by investment advisors (salespeople) that had not done their due diligence and ignored red flags about the Madoff product (Steklow, 2009). Most prosecutions for misconduct come down to lying, cheating, or deception in a specific transaction by an individual. Regulatory bodies and prosecutors do very little to restore an ethical culture in an organization where the individuals were encouraged or provided incentives to engage in misconduct. If an organization has a culture of opaque decision making, lack of accountability, unreliable operating systems with rewards for performance, the stage has been set for misconduct.

To handle the risks of the sales organization, risk management must be enterprise-wide. Linkages to stakeholders' expectations must exist, as well as to the expectations of boards of directors, senior executives, and other constituencies. An emerging business practice known as Enterprise Risk Management (ERM) can provide a top–down, holistic approach to effective risk management. The goal of ERM is to make sure that the organization will achieve its objectives by managing risk within the stakeholders' range of acceptability for risk (Beasley & Frigo, 2007). If ERM is implemented correctly, it not only protects stakeholders but will create stakeholder value as well. ERM differs from traditional risk management approaches that tend to examine risk in isolation, viewing it as a silo or stove pipe (Beasley & Frigo, 2007). Using a traditional approach, risks managed by the sales function do not address the danger of risks in other areas of the enterprise, including strategic risks. Addressing risks within the sales function does not affect outside areas, and therefore does not mitigate all risks. ERM, on the other hand, seeks to consider the interactive effects of various threats with the goal of balancing an enterprise portfolio. ERM presses to ensure that areas of an organization are within an acceptable range, or appetite, for risk (Beasley & Frigo, 2007).

An example from the recent financial meltdown underscores the failure to utilize ERM on the part of many companies. Consider AIG and its financial products unit that sold credit default swaps, a derivative that provided a form of insurance, without carefully assessing the risk to the entire enterprise. While highly profitable, this financial instrument carried great risk to the entire organization. Nevertheless, the unit offered lucrative rewards to employees for selling the product to banks, hedge funds, and other financial institutions that needed insurance protection for the collateralized debt obligations they bought from organizations such as Freddie Mac. Even after warnings from the CEO, the financial products unit of AIG ignored risks for the entire organization in the drive to create personal financial rewards and higher profits (Loomis, 2009). Ultimately, the actions of the sales unit affected all areas of the business. In enterprise-wide risk management, on the other hand, risk is not viewed as simply financial, but also takes into account nonfinancial risk elements such as ethical risk, and states that consideration of these risks also needs to be integrated across an enterprise.

Developing an effective framework for enterprise-wide sales ethics

Because organizations of all types are increasingly accountable to an expanding number of stakeholders, not merely shareholders and customers, new approaches are being developed to incorporate ethics and social responsibility. Issues such as sustainability; data privacy; and health and welfare of consumers are important to many stakeholder groups. The Open Compliance Ethics Group (OCEG) has suggested that the notion of principled performance be expanded to include economic performance and corporate social responsibility (Mitchell, 2009). Principled performance includes both financial and nonfinancial elements and provides the company with guidelines and boundaries for its operations, including mandated regulations such as laws; core processes often called best practices; and voluntary actions, including its values and external promises. Principled performance means defining what is appropriate for a firm, then working to always proceed in a manner in keeping with those findings so as to create and protect value, as well as to address uncertainty and risk. Principled performance also establishes boundaries for employee conduct. It should extend the traditional shareholder view of performance to address other stakeholder interests and help an organization to secure long-term success. The OCEG has developed a number of enterprise processes that help to create integrated governance, risk management, and compliance programs (Mitchell, 2009). This approach is consistent with the popular concept of the Triple Bottom Line. The Triple Bottom Line captures a spectrum of values and criteria for measuring organizational success, including economic, environmental, and social factors.

Figure 1 identifies an overall approach to managing sales ethics through an organizational process. The first stage involves a commitment to SO, and determining

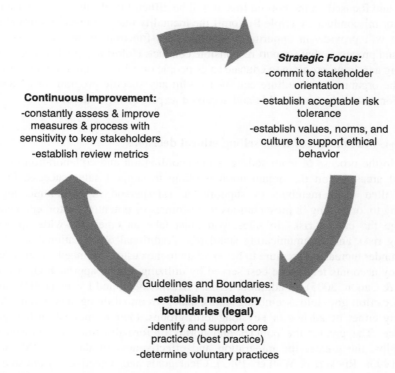

Figure 1.   Framework for enterprise-wide sales ethics.

values and norms that drive ethical behavior. Establishing acceptable risk tolerance related to stakeholders helps in identifying appropriate risk thresholds of each group. This first stage helps to understand and create an ethical culture. The second stage involves identifying the activities and processes for ethical behavior, the legal mandates relevant in the organization, as well as assessing industry-wide best practices in managing risk and employee behavior. In addition, at this stage, the organization identifies areas of interest to stakeholders that through voluntary actions can support corporate social responsibility. In the third stage, a continuous improvement system is developed to identify risks that are not being properly managed through the current process. Key metrics and systems are developed to apprise top management and key decision makers of changes in expectations and behavior which need to be addressed in revisions to this process.

The implementation of SO requires effective corporate governance, understanding risks, ethics, and compliance, as well as effective internal controls. The corporate culture has to provide systems and processes to manage ethics and compliance. Without enterprise-wide commitment to SO, the sales function in an unethical organizational culture will be a silo in a sea of sharks. The failure to identify key stakeholder groups could result in a failure to address important risks. In addition to a strong commitment to ethics and responsibility, resources and a sense of urgency to act are required. Gaining feedback from relevant stakeholders is necessary when formulating a successful corporate strategy.

Many of the rewards that are provided to the sales force are approved and encouraged by top management and the board of directors. The nature of a sales orientation is to provide incentives for the salesperson and sales managers to reach sales objectives. The failure to achieve sales objectives will result in fewer financial rewards and often termination of employment. In an organization in which the mentality is exclusively 'sales oriented' and focused on the bottom line, it will be difficult to eliminate the pressures and rewards for misconduct. A Triple Bottom Line mentality that is embraced throughout the enterprise will provide an opportunity for the sales function to become a part of the systems and processes that support responsible conduct. Unfortunately, it is not as easy as conducting a training program to educate sales people on ethics or creating a sales code of ethics. The organizational culture can overwhelm any specific program or policy if the rewards for misconduct are visible and accepted as part of the culture.

Enterprise-wide nature of team selling ethical decisions

Inherent in the process of team selling is the coordination and collaboration of various functional areas within the organization working to support sales success. Providing highly skilled team members to support the salesperson in communicating with, responding to, or joining in presentations to customers or potential customers means that to manage the ethical risks in sales, you must take an enterprise-wide approach to evaluating risks and communicating standards. Traditional organizational structures in sales are under increasing pressure to better adapt to the customers' needs (Piercy & Lane, 2003). Key accounts tend to be best served by utilizing a team approach (Jones, Dixon, Chonko, & Canon, 2005). In addition, Henke, Krachenberg, and Lyons (1993) note that much more effort goes into assembling teams, than goes into training those teams. As these teams may either be ad hoc or key long-term groups, their formalization has strategic importance. The greater the policies and norms of formalization that influence team relationships, the greater the integration and effectiveness of the team (Moenaert & Souder, 1990; Ruekert & Walker, 1987). Clear goals and objectives to the sales force result in greater levels of cooperation and lower levels of conflict between functional areas within the organization (Norburn, Dunn, Birley, & Boxx, 1995). Therefore, enterprise-wide risk management mechanisms would support increased efficiency and effectiveness as they clarified risks and organizational expectations related to those risks.

As sales organizations increase their reliance on sales teams, the ethical culture of the organization may have more impact on ethical decisions than the prevailing sales ethics subculture. Collaborative understanding and commitment to adhering to enterprise-wide risk management, ethical norms, values and behaviors will be necessary to avoid conflict between team members. As products become more technical and more complex, the sales team will be required to work with other divisions of the firm to create solutions for the customer (Jones et al., 2005). Different attitudes toward ethics have the potential to create conflicts and the possibility of misconduct. The ethical conflicts in the selling team can be intensified when selling to a buying center. These interactions can be person-to-person or selling team-to-buying team. While there is this opportunity for the buying firm and selling firm to create a collaborative long-term relationship, the selling firm and sales team must be in touch with the buying team's ethical standards and culture. Since each organization will have a somewhat different ethical culture, expectations and perceptions about ethics, trust, transparency, and fairness can be different.

If the sales team includes representatives of engineering, R&D, supply chain, and other functions, it is important to have an enterprise-wide consensus on ethical behavior. This enterprise-wide consensus will only occur through organizational ethics programs and processes that create an ethical culture, and will stem from viewing the components of customer interaction as a holistic understanding about ethics in the context of complex interactions (Mattsson, 2008). All team members should be aware of the level of risk that can be acquired, as well as ethical values and norms and compliance standards. Once team members from cross-functional areas understand and accept the ethical culture, then the stage is set for critical thinking and collaboration to resolve new ethical dilemmas. There will never be sufficient rules, policies, and compliance standards to anticipate new emerging ethical issues. Developing a team awareness that considers ethical issues and stakeholders will allow team members to rely on each other and engage in constructive debate to resolve issues.

Conclusions

Based on our framework, organizations need to address sales force ethics from a strategic, enterprise-wide perspective. Most major ethical misconduct in sales stems from systematic failure related to isolating the sales function and creating incentives and rewards for taking marginal yet excessive risks. Organizational pressure for financial performance can be translated into unrealistic expectations from sales. The average tenure of a Chief Marketing Officer is a mere 22.9 months, indicating the strong performance pressure on this position. When performance expectations vary among top executives, there is greater organizational-wide opportunity for wrongdoing (Brand Autopsy, 2004). Approaching sales ethics from the individual perspective ignores the importance of stakeholder risk assessment and the influence of organizational cultures and the sales subculture. While there will be rogue salespersons or 'lone wolves', a principles based ethics and compliance program can minimize the number of individuals that engage in misconduct.

Starting with a strategic SO it is possible to assess and respond to the most visible and relevant stakeholder communities. Organizational values and norms can dictate modes of behavior that not only meet, but exceed stakeholder expectations. Clear organizational values and norms are needed to select among conflicting stakeholder demands. Understanding ethical decision making in an organizational context is necessary to develop an overall strategy to establish systems and processes to obtain desired ethical outcomes. Both individual and organizational factors that influence ethical decision making must be considered in establishing acceptable ranges for risk taking and internal controls.

Ethical decision making in sales requires an understanding and integration with an enterprise-wide ethics initiative. Because of cross-functional involvement in sales, especially in key account management and team selling, excessive foci on the individual salesperson or viewing the sales area as in control of all ethical outcomes have many limitations. Unless both the organization and the sales area have the same SO, they will fail to identify risks that create important ethical issues. A SO embraces both enterprise-wide values and behaviors as well as sales behaviors. All organizational participants need to be continuously aware of, and act positively to address current and emerging issues. Based on a societal emphasis on transparency, the failure to consider all significant stakeholders can lead to ethical conflict, diminished reputation, and legal issues. When both the enterprise and the sales function listen to stakeholder concerns, they can resolve and avoid ethical mistakes. The tangible benefits of enterprise-wide stakeholder perspective include improved financial performance, customer loyalty, collaborative partnerships, and improved reputation. It is important to go beyond basic regulatory requirements by integrating SO into the organization, marketing strategy, as well as the sales strategy.

Enterprise-wide risk management is a holistic view of risk that establishes boundaries and a range of acceptability for risk. Based on the global financial industry meltdown, failure to effectively manage risk will become more important in the future. Enterprise risk management differs from traditional risk management in that it considers risk across the organization, versus in isolation. The sales function may be focused on the risks of salespersons paying bribes, fixing prices, or conflicts of interest. A holistic approach considers the risks which occur outside the sales function.

A corporate culture creates principled performance by establishing values and norms that create boundaries for activities; including required nonnegotiable compliance, core practices, a commitment to excel, and allow for voluntary contributions to integrity. The Triple Bottom Line, which includes criteria for measuring organizational success such as economic, environmental, and social factors, provides a useful assessment of implementation. Too often, the sales force operates in an organizational environment where their role and rewards are all focused on a single, financial, bottom line. The incentives for performance overshadow concerns for a balanced stakeholder perspective. When the rewards are placed into a one-dimensional perspective, the possibility of focusing on transactional relationships that take care of short run requirements is created.

Future research should focus on the SO concept, its benefits, and link to sales ethical performance. Studies that compare the SO, MO, and customer orientations as factors that influence sales ethics could provide an increased understanding of the strategic management of sales performance. While research has linked SO with financial performance of the firm, investigating the relationship of SO to sales performance could provide directions for developing incentives and a holistic evaluation of sales performance. Studies to determine industry-wide ethical risks and risk tolerance can assist in managing organizational and sales ethics risks. Classifying mandatory (legal) requirements, core best practices, and appropriate voluntary activities to support sales ethics could be beneficial. Ethics audits, assessments, and metrics to gauge performance could assist in continuous improvement. The strategic management of sales ethics will continue to consider individuals that operate independently and require compliance and internal control systems to prevent misconduct.

References

Barrett, W.P., & Novack, J. (2009, February 16). Never cheat a cheater. *Forbes*, p. 38.

Beasley, M.S., & Frigo, M.L. (2007). Strategic risk management: Creating and protecting value. *Strategic Finance, 88*(11), 25–31.

Bellizzi, J.A., & Bristol, T. (2005). Supervising the unethical selling behavior of top sales performers: Assessing the impact of social desirability bias. *Journal of Business Ethics, 57*(4), 377–388.

Bellizzi, J.A., & Hasty, R.W. (2003). Supervising unethical sales force behavior: How strong is the tendency to treat top performers leniently? *Journal of Business Ethics, 43*(4), 337–351.

Bhattacharya, C.B., & Korschun, D. (2008). Stakeholder marketing: Beyond the four Ps and the customer. *Journal of Public Policy & Marketing, 27*(1), 113–116.

Blodgett, J.G., Lu, L.-C., Rose, G.M., & Vitell, S.J. (2001). Ethical sensitivity to stakeholder interests: A cross-cultural comparison. *Journal of the Academy of Marketing Science, 29*(2), 190–202.

Brand Autopsy. (2004). *The shrinking tenure of CMOs*. Retrieved February 6, 2009 from http://brandautopsy.typepad.com/brandautopsy/2004/07/the_shrinking_t.html

Brewer, L., Chandler, R., & Ferrell, O.C. (2006). *Managing risks for corporate integrity: How to survive an ethical misconduct disaster*. Mason, OH: Thomson Higher Education.

British Petroleum (BP). *External relationships*. Retrieved February 6, 2009 from http://www.bp.com/sectiongenericarticle.do?categoryId=9002637&contentId=7005208

Cohen, J.B. & Reed, A., II (2006). A Multiple Pathway Anchoring and Adjustment (MPAA) model of attitude generation and recruitment. *Journal of Consumer Research, 33*(1), 1–15.

Day, G.S. (1994). The capabilities of market-driven organizations. *Journal of Marketing, 58*(4), 37–52.

Deshpandé, R., Farley, J.U., & Webster, F.E. (1993). Corporate culture, customer orientation, and innovativeness in Japanese firms: A quadrad analysis. *Journal of Marketing, 57*(1), 23–27.

Dubinsky, A.J., & Loken, B. (1989). Analyzing ethical decision making in marketing. *Journal of Business Research, 19*(2), 83–107.

Ethisphere Magazine. (2008). European Commission fines 'paraffin mafia' €676 million. *Resource guide: Antitrust/business practices* (global) (4th quarter), p. 70.

Farrell, M.A. (2005). The effect of a market-oriented organisational culture on sales-force behaviour and attitudes. *Journal of Strategic Marketing, 13*(4), 261–273.

Ferrell, O.C., Fraedrich, J., & Ferrell, L. (2008). *Business ethics: Ethical decision making and cases* (7th ed.). Boston, MA: Houghton Mifflin Company.

Ferrell, O.C., & Gresham, L.G. (1985). A contingency framework for understanding ethical decision making in marketing. *Journal of Marketing, 49*(3), 87–96.

Ferrell, O.C., Gresham, L.G., & Fraedrich, J. (1989). A synthesis of ethical decision models for marketing. *Journal of Macromarketing, 9*(2), 55–64.

Ferrell, O.C., Johnston, M., & Ferrell, L. (2007). A framework for personal selling and sales management ethical decision making. *Journal of Personal Selling & Sales Management, 4*(27), 291–299.

Freeman, R.E. (1984). *Strategic management: A stakeholder approach*. Boston, MA: Pitman.

Frooman, J. (1999). Stakeholder influence strategies. *Academy of Management Review, 24*(2), 191–205.

Henke, J.W., Krachenberg, A.R., & Lyons, T.E. (1993). Cross-functional teams: Good concepts, poor implementation. *Journal of Product Innovation Management, 10*(3), 216–229.

Hunt, S.D., & Vitell, S.J. (1986). A general theory of marketing ethics. *Journal of Macromarketing, 6*(1), 5–16.

Hunt, S.D., & Vitell, S.J. (2006). The general theory of marketing ethics: A revision and three questions. *Journal of Macromarketing, 26*(2), 143–153.

Ingram, T.N., LaForge, R.W., & Schwepker, C.H., Jr. (2007). Salesperson ethical decision making: The impact of sales leadership and sales management control strategy. *Journal of Personal Selling & Sales Management, 27*(4), 301–316.

Jaramillo, F., Ladik, D.M., Marshall, G.W., & Mulki, J.P. (2007). A meta-analysis of the relationship between Sales Orientation–Customer Orientation (SOCO) and salesperson job performance. *Journal of Business and Industrial Marketing*, 25(5), 302–310.

Jones, E., Dixon, A.L., Chonko, L.B., & Canon, J.P. (2005). Key accounts and team selling: A review, framework, and research agenda. *Journal of Personal Selling and Sales Management*, 25(2), 181–198.

Loe, T., Ferrell, L., & Mansfield, P. (2000). A review of empirical studies assessing ethical decision making in business. *Journal of Business Ethics*, 25(3), 185–204.

Loomis, C. (2009, January 19). AIG: The company that came to dinner. *Fortune*, 70–78.

Maignan, I., & Ferrell, O.C. (2004). Corporate social responsibility and marketing: An integrative framework. *Journal of the Academy of Marketing Science*, 32(1), 3–19.

Maignan, I., Hult, T., Ferrell, O.C., & Gonzalez, T. (2009). Stakeholder orientation: Development and testing of an expanded framework for marketing. MSU working paper.

Mattsson, J. (2008). Strategy by bottom–up abstractions of the customer interface. *Journal of Strategic Marketing*, 15(5), 391–399.

McClaren, N. (2000). Ethics in personal selling and sales management: A review of the literature focusing on empirical findings and conceptual foundations. *Journal of Business Ethics*, 27(3), 285–303.

Mitchell, R.K., Agle, B.R., & Wood, D.J. (1997). Toward a theory of stakeholder identification and salience: Defining the principle of who and what really counts. *Academy of Management Review*, 22(4), 853–886.

Mitchell, S.L. (2009). *A pathway to Principled Performance®: The OCEG framework approach to integrated GRC*. Retrieved February 3, 2009, from OCEG Online, http://www.oceg.org/Details/20055

Moenaert, R.K., & Souder, W.E. (1990). An information transfer model for integrating marketing and R&D in personnel in new product development projects. *Journal of Product Innovation Management*, 7(2), 91–107.

Narver, J.C., & Slater, S.F. (1990). The effect of market orientation on business profitability. *Journal of Marketing*, 54(4), 20–35.

Norburn, D., Dunn, M.G., Birley, S., & Boxx, R.W. (1995). Corporate values and the marketing concept: Examining interfunctional relationships. *Journal of Strategic Marketing*, 3(4), 215–232.

Piercy, N.F., & Lane, N. (2003). Transformation of the traditional sales force: Imperatives for intelligence, interface, and integration. *Journal of Marketing Management*, 5(6), 563–583.

Piercy, N., & Lane, N. (2007). Ethical and moral dimensions associated with strategic relationships between business-to-business buyers and sellers. *Journal of Business Ethics*, 72(1), 87–102.

Polonsky, M.J. (1996). Stakeholder management and the stakeholder matrix: Potential strategic marketing tools. *Journal of Market-Focused Management*, 1(3), 209–229.

Robin, D.P., Gordon, G., Jordan, C., & Reidenback, R.E. (1996). The empirical performance of cognitive moral development in predicting behavioral intent. *Business Ethics Quarterly*, 6(4), 493–515.

Rowley, T.J. (1997). Moving beyond dyadic ties: A network theory of stakeholder influences. *Academy of Management Review*, 22(4), 887–910.

Ruekert, R.W., & Walker, O.C. (1987). Marketing's interface with other functional units: A conceptual framework and empirical evidence. *Journal of Marketing*, 51(1), 1–19.

Sen, S., Bhattacharya, C.B., & Korschun, D. (2006). The role of corporate social responsibility in strengthening multiple stakeholder relationships: A field experiment. *Journal of the Academy of Marketing Science*, 34(2), 158–166.

Singhapakdi, A., & Vitell, S.J. (1992). Marketing ethics: Sales professionals versus other marketing professionals. *Journal of Personal Selling and Sales Management*, 12(4), 27–38.

Steklow, S. (2009, January 28). In echoes of Madoff, Ponzi cases proliferate. *Wall Street Journal*. Retrieved January 31, 2009, from http://online.wsj.com/article/SB123310397888922265.html

Wotruba, T.R. (1990). A comprehensive framework for the analysis of ethical behavior, with a focus on sales organizations. *Journal of Professional Selling & Sales Management*, 10(Spring), 29–42.

Strategic sales organizations: transformation challenges and facilitators within the sales–marketing interface

Avinash Malshe

Opus College of Business, University of St Thomas, Mail #TMH343, 1000 LaSalle Ave, Minneapolis MN 55403, USA

As business firms embrace the emerging strategic sales organizations, they need to be mindful of the intra-organizational factors that may facilitate or challenge this transformation and its related strategic imperatives. Using depth-interview data collected from 38 sales and marketing executives, this study highlights the similarities and differences in sales and marketing personnel's perceptions about the role they and their counterparts may play in the strategic process. Drawing on these insights, it then brings forth the 'role-related' and 'process-related' factors that may facilitate and challenge strategic imperatives associated with the new sales paradigm. This paper thus highlights the nuances of the role expectations within the sales–marketing interface, and its impact on strategic imperatives that may determine the firm's movement toward a strategic customer management philosophy.

When marketing and sales functions work well together, they can create and deliver superior customer value. Hence, it is crucial for seamless value creation and delivery that the sales–marketing interface remains frictionless (Dewsnap & Jobber, 2000, 2002; Guenzi & Troilo, 2007). Extant research suggests that in many business organizations, marketing is typically in charge of strategy creation activity, while sales is entrusted with the task of strategy implementation (Kotler, Rackham, & Krishnaswamy, 2006; Rouziès et al., 2005). Recent advances in our understanding of this phenomenon however, suggest that the changing business landscape and newly emerging competitive threats are requiring firms to rethink the role sales organizations may play in the strategy creation and implementation processes (Ingram, 2004; Leigh & Marshall, 2001; Piercy & Lane, 2003).

Specifically, scholars have argued that in future, firms must not look at their sales organizations as pure 'executors' of marketing strategy, but they must embrace sales organizations that will shoulder important strategic decision-making responsibilities with marketing; that is, the strategic sales organizations. Relatedly, Piercy (2006) and Piercy and Lane (2003) suggest that as business firms prepare for the emergence of the strategic sales organizations, they must consider five important imperatives of this transformation: the need for integration across sales and marketing, involving sales force in strategic process, capturing and using the intelligence generated by salespeople, effectively marketing the customer internally within the organization, and aligning sales structures and processes with the broader business strategy.

While this transformation presents exciting opportunities, firms must keep in mind that certain intra-organizational factors may facilitate or challenge the emergence of a strategic sales organization and its resultant imperatives. Given that sales and marketing functions are ideally jointly involved in the strategy making and execution process, and that the sales–marketing interface has been known to be acrimonious (Dewsnap & Jobber, 2000; Homburg, Ove, & Krohmer, 2008; Lorge, 1999), studying the likely facilitating factors and challenges to this transformation through the sales–marketing interface perspective can offer a greater insight into this emerging phenomenon.

Two specific areas need attention in this regard. First, as extant research has shown, sales and marketing functions have different orientations, foci, and thought worlds (Cespedes, 1996; Homburg & Jensen, 2007; Strahle, Spiro, & Acito, 1996). Hence, individuals within these functions may hold different notions about what role they and their counterparts are supposed to play in the strategic process (e.g. salespeople may believe that they should assume a strategic role within the firm; however, marketers may not view them as strategic partners and not offer them opportunities to get extensively involved in strategy-creation activity). A 'mismatch' on these role expectations of self and the other function can create a challenge for firms as the sales organization's role becomes more pronounced. Second, the emergence of the strategic sales organization may require sales and marketing personnel to rethink their traditional strategy creation and implementation processes. As a result, it may require each function to alter its involvement and also the specific activities they would perform in these processes.

In summary, when the transformation of the sales organization is viewed through the sales–marketing interface lens, two questions need greater inquiry: (1) What are the similarities and differences between sales and marketing in their expectations of the role each function should play in the strategic process? (2) How will these differences (similarities) in the *role expectations* of self and the other function create challenges (or serve as facilitators) for each function as they prepare for the emergence of a strategic sales organization?

Using qualitative data collected from 38 depth interviews with marketing and sales professionals, this paper seeks to answer the above research questions. Specifically, it identifies the role expectations of each department for itself and its counterpart thereby highlighting the overlaps and differences in their perceptions. Drawing on these insights, this paper then highlights the 'role-related' and 'process-related' factors that may facilitate and challenge strategic imperatives associated with the new sales paradigm. Together, this paper thus highlights the nuances of the role expectations within the sales–marketing interface, and its impact on strategic imperatives that may determine the firm's movement toward a 'strategic customer management' philosophy (Piercy, 2006).

This paper is organized as follows. First, I review the literature on the sales–marketing interface and the changing nature of sales organizations within business firms. Next, I discuss the study methodology. It is followed by the presentation of study findings. This paper ends with highlighting the theoretical contributions, managerial implications, limitations of this study, and suggestions regarding future research directions.

Literature review

The sales–marketing interface

The Marketing Science Institute workshop on interfunctional interfaces identified the conflict between marketing and sales as one of the critical areas needing attention more than a decade ago (Webster & Montgomery, 1997). Nonetheless, it is very recently that scholars have started paying greater attention to the marketing–sales interface (e.g. Homburg et al., 2008; Kotler et al., 2006). Further, barring a few exceptions, studies in this area are largely conceptual (Rouziès et al., 2005).

Extant literature proposes that sales and marketing activities are ideally closely coordinated, with salespeople collecting market information, conveying it to their marketing colleagues, and marketing creating customized products and programs in response to the market insight (Dewsnap & Jobber, 2000; Rouziès et al., 2005). Over the years however, scholars have noted that the marketing–sales interface is not always harmonious and constructive. Further, under-communication, underperformance, and over-complaining have been shown to characterize this interface (Beverland, Steel, & Dapiran, 2006; Carpenter, 1992; Cespedes, 1993; Lorge, 1999; Strahle et al., 1996).

In an effort to understand this interface better, scholars have investigated disparate phenomena. Scholars highlight that major differences between sales and marketing may be a function of cultural mismatch, interfunctional conflict, differences in thought worlds, and different perspectives toward the marketplace (Beverland et al., 2006; Dawes & Massey, 2005; Homburg & Jensen, 2007; Piercy, 2006). Further, scholars have noted that lack of cooperation and communication, turf battles, differences in goal orientation, lack of role clarity, misalignment of strategic objectives, and poor coordination may hamper development of a cordial rapport between sales and marketing (Colletti & Chonko, 1997; Hutt, 1995; Strahle et al., 1996).

Acknowledging the stormy relationship between the two functions, scholars have explored avenues to bring these two functions closer. Specific suggestions include aligning strategic capabilities, enhancing interfunctional coordination, cooperation, and collabor-ation, and encouraging joint participation in strategic activities (Cespedes, 1993; Guenzi & Troilo, 2006; Ingram, 2004; LeMeunier-Fitz-Hugh & Piercy, 2007; Matthyssens & Johnston, 2006). Synchronization and coordination of activities may be achieved through establishing clear lines of responsibility and authority for various strategy-related tasks. Collaboration is a function of how well each function contributes its resources to joint activities and whether there is a cordial, relationship between the two functions. Scholars have also highlighted the need for integrating the two functions in that each function supports the activities of the other and that the two groups have equally vested interests in the outcomes of their activities (Le Meunier-FitzHugh & Piercy, 2007). Other avenues such as enhancing interdepartmental communication so that they key information is optimally shared in terms of frequency, modality, timeliness, and bidirectionality, as well as bridging cultural differences, have also been recommended (Beverland et al., 2006).

Changing nature of the sales organization

While the extant sales–marketing interface literature primarily describes salespeople as strategy implementers, in recent years, academics and industry watchers alike have noted that sales organizations across many industries are undergoing an unparalleled transformation (Challey Group, 1998; Leigh & Marshall, 2001; Piercy, 2006; Piercy & Lane, 2003). The major change that these sources identify is that sales organizations are no longer the executors of the marketing strategy alone; they are playing an increasingly important role in strategy conceptualization and planning activities.

There are many reasons why sales organizations are increasingly assuming a strategic role, for example, pressure from ever demanding customers to deliver superior customer value, changing competitive landscape, emergence of new business models, and so on

(Piercy & Lane, 2003), which have replaced the traditional sales processes and given rise to the new ones. Leigh and Marshall (2001) observe that firms have started viewing issues such as customer selection, knowledge of and access to customers, as well as customer relationship management as strategic and that these are no longer relegated to the tactical domain of sales management. Needless to say, sales organizations, owing to their proximity to customers are increasingly feeling the need to move away from their traditional order-taking roles to more of a customer relationship management role wherein they create, nurture, and maintain long-term customer relationships and actively participate in the strategy-making processes (Ingram, 2004; Ingram, LaForge, & Leigh, 2002).

In a thought piece published recently, Piercy (2006), while highlighting the shift in sales organization's role within business firms proposes that we are seeing an emergence of strategic sales organizations. He notes that as firms get ready to embrace this new paradigm, they need to be mindful of its strategic imperatives: involvement of sales organization in core strategic decision-making processes, integration across sales and marketing so that the functional boundaries are blurred and customer focus is sharpened, internal marketing of customer needs within the organizational boundaries, creation of a superior infrastructure that will allow for alignment of sales structures and processes with the overall business strategy of the firm, and utilization of the intelligence developed by the sales force. Similar ideas have been put forward by Le Meunier-FitzHugh and Piercy (2006), and Piercy and Lane (2003), who exhort firms to view sales activities as strategic customer management activities, tap into the crucial market intelligence salespeople generate, and integrate sales force in strategy creation and customer portfolio decision-making processes.

Next, I discuss my study methodology.

Methodology

Sample and data collection

Given the lack of extant knowledge and guiding theories in this area, I used a discovery-oriented, theories-in-use approach in this study. This approach is consistent with the emerging body of research using qualitative methodology to study organizational phenomena (Flint, Woodruff, & Gardial, 2002; Tuli, Kohli, & Bharadwaj, 2007). I used the theoretical sampling technique (Strauss & Corbin, 1998) in this study, which allows for sampling respondents in such a way so that the researcher may maximize the discovery of variations among concepts (Creswell, 2007). I approached 45 sales and marketing professionals and requested their participation in the study. Seven declined the interview request for confidentiality reasons resulting in a sample size of 38 professionals. The informant profile is offered in Table 1, which highlights sample diversity in terms of companies and industries represented, as well as job titles of my respondents. Each informant had been in his/her current job for at least three years and hence was well versed with the research topic. Informant companies were comparable in size and annual sales. All of them operated in business to business environments.

The interviews were discovery-oriented (Deshpande, 1983); the shortest being 40 minutes and the longest lasting over 75 minutes. I conducted the interviews at a place and time convenient to the informants. Consistent with McCracken's (1988) suggested interview protocol, I began the interviews with a few minutes of idle chatter so as make the informants feel comfortable with me. Further, the opening questions were simple and informational; about the firm, its products and the informant's background. Once I was certain that the informant felt comfortable conversing with me that I launched into the 'grand tour' questions.

Table 1. Informant profile.

#	Name	Sex	Level	Industry	Job title
1	Abigail	F	Senior	Telecom	CMO
2	Ashton	M	Middle	IT	Regional marketing manager
3	Carie	F	Junior	Telecom	Sales executive
4	Cheryl	F	Middle	Electronics	Sales manager–Midwest
5	Dan	M	Senior	IT	VP–Sales
6	Dave	M	Junior	Pharmaceuticals	Sales representative
7	Eanaa	F	Senior	Publishing	Marketing manager
8	Elizabeth	F	Junior	IT	Sales executive
9	Forest	M	Senior	Healthcare	Dir of sales–SBU
10	Ginger	F	Middle	Publishing	Marketing manager
11	JB	F	Senior	Engineering products	VP–Sales
12	Jeev	M	Senior	Engineering products	Marketing manager
13	Jennifer	F	Junior	Electronics	Sales representative
14	Jess	F	Middle	Telecom	Field marketing manager
15	Jessey	M	Middle	IT	Marketing executive
16	Jil	F	Junior	Telecom	Sales representative
17	Jim	M	Middle	Pharmaceuticals	Account manager
18	Joe	M	Junior	Pharmaceuticals	Sales representative
19	Juliette	F	Middle	Materials	District sales manager
20	Ken	M	Middle	Engineering products	Sales manager–East coast
21	KK	M	Senior	Healthcare	National sales manager
22	Kristi	F	Junior	Industrial products	Brand executive
23	Lesley	F	Junior	Engineering products	Sales manager–Institutional sales
24	Liam	M	Middle	IT	Account manager
25	Mac	M	Junior	Electronics	District sales manager
26	Manny	M	Junior	Engineering products	Manager–Marketing
27	Marshall	M	Senior	Materials	CMO
28	Martina	F	Senior	Industrial products	Assistant VP–Marketing
29	Meg	F	Middle	IT	District sales manager
30	Pamela	F	Middle	IT	Regional marketing manager
31	Rebecca	M	Junior	Healthcare	Sales representative
32	Rita	F	Middle	Pharmaceuticals	Field marketing manager
33	Roger	M	Junior	IT	Sales representative
34	Ron	M	Middle	Publishing	Regional sales manager
35	Sam	M	Middle	Electronics	Regional marketing manager
36	Steve	M	Senior	Healthcare	Dir–Sales of SBU
37	Trevor	M	Junior	Engineering products	Sales executive
38	Victoria	F	Senior	Materials	VP–Sales

I used a structured set of questions for the interviews (see Appendix 1). Nonetheless, I allowed the informants to guide the flow and content of the discussion. I solicited examples and clarifications as they spoke. This dialog provided informants an opportunity to correct anything that I misunderstood or offer additional explanation. Throughout the interview process, I tried to maintain objectivity to reduce interviewer-induced bias (McCracken, 1988). I audio-taped all interviews and transcribed them verbatim. I stopped interviewing upon reaching theoretical saturation, when no new insights were emerging from the interviews (Strauss & Corbin, 1998).

Data analysis

I managed the interview notes using QSR International's NVivo software. I coded the data iteratively, which is consistent with the qualitative inquiry practices. I constantly reviewed the interview transcripts as the data collection progressed to identify emerging themes, which provided directions for the subsequent data collection. The themes were constantly refined based on subsequent interview data. At the beginning, open coding helped me identify important concepts and their properties, and group them into categories (Corley & Gioia, 2004). The focus at this stage was on the 'in-vivo' conceptual codes – that is, the language used by the informants (Strauss & Corbin, 1990). In the next step, axial coding helped me identify relationships between and among these first-order categories and come up with higher-order themes. In the last step, these higher-order themes helped me understand the emergent framework. Though my coding techniques were non-linear and recursive (Corley & Gioia, 2004), I avoided forcing emergent patterns into preconceived categories (Gummesson, 2003). In the interest of space, I do not provide a table highlighting the in-vivo codes and higher-order themes. I evaluated the data insights and themes on three criteria: (1) applicability of idea beyond a specific industry; (2) how frequently informants mentioned an idea/theme; and (3) insightfulness. Hence, I focus on novel ideas that are not industry specific, and not explicitly discussed in literature (Tuli et al., 2007).

I insured the analytical rigor using steps suggested by Lincoln and Guba (1985). First, I managed my data using the NVivo software. It helped me flawlessly maintain informant contact records, interview transcripts, field notes, and other related documents, as they were collected. This was further verified by an outside experienced researcher, who went through the field notes, interview protocols, coding schemes, and random samples of interview transcripts to assess the plausibility of my conclusions. Second, I randomly selected 22 informant interviews and asked two independent judges to evaluate my coding. These judges had prior experience with qualitative data analysis. The proportional reduction in loss based on the judges' agreement or disagreement with each of my codes in these interviews was 0.86, which is well above the 0.70 cut-off level (e.g. Rust & Cooil, 1994). Last, I verified my interpretations and the accuracy of the findings using member checks (Creswell, 2007) where I shared the findings with 12 randomly selected study participants and asked them to offer their views on my data interpretations and the credibility of the findings. Next, I discuss the findings of this study.

Findings

I begin this section by presenting what sales and marketing professionals mentioned their expectations were of each function's role in the strategic process. Drawing on these insights, I next highlight the factors that may help/challenge marketers and salespeople respectively, as they prepare to embrace the emerging strategic sales organization.

How marketers view themselves

My data suggest that marketers believe that they are, and should remain at the center of firm's strategic activities. As such, they consider themselves to be the 'strategic hub' within the firm that thinks long-term. They further believe that they are in the best position to interact with multiple departments such as R&D, finance, pricing, and so on, and insure that their perspectives are adequately represented in the strategic process. Ron suggests:

> I see marketing as sort of the center of the universe, to some extent. You'll have finance saying, 'this is what we can afford to do or not do'. You'll have manufacturing saying, 'this is what we can or can't make'. You'll have engineering saying, 'here's what we can or can't design', and sales saying, 'here's what we can sell or can't sell'. Marketing has to weigh all of that out and make the call ... not listening too closely to any one discipline. If they do,

they won't do the right thing. If they ignore any of the disciplines, they won't do the right thing either. (Ron, Marketing)

That marketing is a crucial strategic function and as such may not be relegated to the sidelines is evidenced in Eanaa's quote:

Marketers think about programs and plans that are different and innovative; something that changes their market ... they are the change agents within the organizations. They're also very strategic and they can sense things from far away ... they have the ability to think outside the box. They don't believe in maintaining the status quo; they want to change things. (Eanaa, Marketing)

My data further indicated that marketers want to remain the key decision-makers within the marketing strategy-making process. While many marketing informants welcomed sales organization's participation in the strategic process, none of them felt that the changing business landscape necessitates a shift in the strategic decision-making power from marketing to sales organizations. Relatedly, while they appreciated sales organization's inputs in strategy making, a majority of them were not excited about the prospect of sharing the decision-making authority with sales. On the contrary, they viewed this as an unwelcome/forced 'delegation of authority'. Pamela's quote is pertinent in this regard:

I think it can be a mistake to delegate your decisions to sales. That would be the thing that I would say to be careful of. Sales has a role to play in the process ... but they should not be the ones making strategic decisions ... it is our task. (Pamela, Marketing)

I further found that marketers did not want to be excessively involved in tactical activities, for example, they were not excited about going out on field visits to close important sales, as and when asked by the salespeople. This was consistent with their perception that marketing is and should be in charge of strategy. Some of my informants mentioned that it was not marketers' job to be 'super sales reps' that would go in the field and assist salespeople close important deals. Jess notes:

It is controversial... It is something that we constantly wrestle with ... I'm a marketing manager, and I don't want to end up being a *super rep* trying to close every deal in every territory ... that's why we have a sales force, and that's where they have the entire sales organization ... it is extremely important to maintain that balance between the two job functions. (Jess, Marketing)

Further, they did not want to be treated as 'on-call' sales support system. Many of my informants noted instances when salespeople called them from the field and asked them to *quickly* create promotional campaigns for certain customer groups. Instances such as these made marketers feel that the long-term thinking behind their marketing strategies is not valued by the sales force, and the implementation happens in a haphazard manner. Abigail notes:

I don't want to be their ready reference that they can call from the field any time they wish ... we provide them information in advance and I would like them to know more about their products and the key decision-makers ... the numbers of customers our reps contact is not very high. So I do expect them to know about customers ... if they don't, that disappoints me. (Abigail, Marketing)

Last, even though marketers did not want to be the 'on-call' support for sales, they were mindful that salespeople depend on them for consistent sales support. They mentioned that marketers must arm salespeople with all the necessary tools. They further mentioned that they are a salesperson's liaison within the organization; relaying the information from the sales organization back into the headquarters and vice-versa. Rita outlines this clearly below:

> I also want to say that if you want to be successful in marketing, you should be the one who is willing and ready to help your salespeople ... it takes a certain kind of personality to be a good marketing manager. I think you do have to be very service-oriented because salespeople depend on you for the field support. (Rita, Marketing)

Overall, this discussion suggests that even in the face of a changing business environment, marketers view themselves as the firm's strategic center. They want to retain the decision-making power; not share it with the sales force. Further, they are mindful that the sales organization depends on them for marketing support. They want to arm salespeople with everything they may need on the field. However they do not want to end up being 'super-reps' closing every sale or 'on-call' sales support.

How marketers view salespeople

Just as marketers have distinct role expectations of themselves; my data indicate that they have a clear mental model of what role the sales organization may play in the strategic process. Specifically, marketers believe that the main task salespeople should be responsible for in the strategic process is strategy implementation. Victoria makes a clear distinction on these lines:

> Most of them [salespeople] are pretty outgoing ... but they are not planners. They will do whatever we ask them to ... they are good at implementation and that is what they should be responsible for (Victoria, Marketing).

Further, marketers expect salespeople to follow the prescribed strategic processes meticulously and stay organized and thoughtful during strategy implementation. Kristi and Jim's quotes below highlight the expectations they have from their sales colleagues:

> It is a challenge for them, many times, to understand that sales does not just involve going out, knocking on a door, making a cold call. There has to be an organized plan that needs to be implemented in order to have a successful sale. (Kristi, Marketing)

> One of the things I have been working very hard to change in this organization is ... I feel that a salesperson needs to have a good solid understanding of a business, before you walk in the door. The salesperson needs to do their homework. When I first came into the organization, people came into the office when they wanted, left when they wanted, did not set up appointments with customers, they did not do work prior to meeting with customers. They would just show up at the customer's door, without a meeting, without a plan, or without knowing much about the customer at all. (Jim, Marketing)

Marketers also expect salespeople to appreciate the long-term perspective behind every marketing strategy. In this regard, they hope that salespeople would act as business managers, who would not only be driven by the monthly/quarterly sales targets and incentives, but also pay attention to the broader factors such as profitability and long-term growth. In this regard, they expected salespeople to be patient, proactive, and focus on customers' long-term needs:

> Our reps do not have a tolerance of dry spells. They tend to deal with very immediate situations. For example, what will help me close this particular deal? They rarely need any reassurance about the long-term prospects of the product or they rarely inquire about their long-term plans for certain products ... except when things are rocky and the products are reaching the end of their lifecycle. So when we do product research, they typically want to solve today's problems that the customer has ... so they tell us that customers do not even imagine that they will have these problems two years out, and therefore they do not feel motivated to think about or talk to their customers about long-term plans. (Martina, Marketing)

My data further revealed that marketers expect salespeople to be cooperative. Specifically, my informants mentioned that salespeople should allow marketers complete access to their customers so that they could directly collect their feedback. Below, Steve expresses frustration over the fact that many times, salespeople in his firms created 'boundaries' around their customers, and expected marketers to not contact their customers directly:

> They are very territorial. When you're trying to get to the customers and test some of your ideas, you sometimes face resistance from the field force ... because they feel they own their customers, and they don't want anybody else talking to their customers ... and they have very, very defined boundaries. (Steve, Marketing)

Last, marketers expect that salespeople would use their connections within the field with other salespeople to exchange market feedback, share success stories, and insure that strategy implementation happens seamlessly:

> It is really fascinating ... they talk to their colleagues around the country. And they couldn't care less about what marketing tells them. They decide amongst themselves how strategies should be implemented ... marketing's directives can go out the door in no time. (Joe, Marketing)

Overall, my data suggested that marketers still believe that the sales organization's main task is strategy implementation and they expect salespeople to be systematic in their implementation approach. They further expect salespeople to learn the bigger strategic picture and understand how their tactical activities fit into the bigger strategic process. Last, they expect salespeople to be cooperative and not create obstacles when marketers try to reach out to their customers and collect market data.

When marketers' perception of their own role is viewed in conjunction with their expectation of what the sales force should be doing, it becomes clear that marketers still make a clear distinction between strategy creation and implementation activities. They view themselves as creators of strategies and view the sales organization as pure 'implementers'.

Next, I highlight how salespeople view themselves and their marketing colleagues.

How salespeople view themselves

Contrary to marketers' expectations of salespeople, my data suggest that they do not view themselves purely as 'implementers' of marketing strategies. On the contrary, they view their role as strategic. My informants from sales mentioned that the scope of their activities is broad – including market sensing, transferring the information to marketing, and facilitating the value delivery process; and hence viewing them as 'implementers' alone is a mistake on marketers' part. Meg has the following to say about this issue:

> It is wrong to think that salespeople are implementers alone ... I think it is critical that marketing include some of our senior reps in their strategic discussions ... we have good ideas and we talk with customers every day ... we can instantly tell you whether your idea is going to fly or not ... we are the eyes and ears of the company. (Meg, Sales)

One of the crucial roles salespeople viewed themselves performing was to be customers' advocate within the firm. As my informants noted, this was an important activity since it insured that the customers' voice was heard within their firms. Specifically, salespeople mentioned that since they are in constant contact with their customers, they have a unique capability of sensing both verbal and nonverbal cues from the customers. Cheryl noted:

> The biggest value that sales can bring to the table is the voice of the customer. We deal with them everyday. So in addition to what they tell us, we also understand tone in their voice ... we meet with them face-to-face and that gives us an opportunity to collect a lot of verbal as

well as nonverbal information. Salespeople can tell you stories behind customer success and failure and that information can be very powerful in terms of creating new products and improving our services. (Cheryl, Sales)

My informants from sales noted that not only were they instrumental in sensing customer requirements, but they also played a role in building long-term customer relationships:

They love to develop relationships with their customers. So they take a long-term view from that standpoint. They may not make an immediate sale, but if they are developing a relationship that is a big value to them (Rebecca, Sales).

Last, my sales informants expressed regret over the fact that marketers expect them to move their focus away from immediate goals to purely long-term objectives. When it came to implementing marketing strategies, they noted that it was difficult for them to keep in mind the bigger picture alone. They also felt that the fast-paced nature of their job made it difficult for them to stay within the boundaries of the prescribed strategy, and follow the tactical guidelines provided by marketers methodically:

Our incentive is against how much we sell, whereas at the end of the year, they [marketers] will be accountable for something else ... we are under the gun every quarter or every week and we have to be performance oriented, we have to get things done and it may be that we have to work around our prescribed processes ... because we do not have the luxury of time as marketers have ... they can take greater degrees of freedom. (Sam, Sales)

Overall, my data revealed that contrary to marketers' expectations, salespeople viewed themselves not as pure 'implementers' of strategy, but as strategic players, whose involvement spans the strategy-making and implementation processes. In addition, while they did not express the urgency to be given decision-making authority, they were insistent that neglecting their voice could hurt strategic outcomes such as sales, market shares, and profitability. They expressed frustration over marketers' expectation that they remain within predefined boundaries during the strategy implementation process. Last, they expressed difficulty over being able to move their focus away from tactical issues and focus purely on long-term aspects of the marketing strategy.

How salespeople view marketers

While my informants from marketing viewed themselves as a 'strategic hub' responsible for long-term marketing strategies, my sales informants contradicted this view by noting that marketers are so far removed from reality that it is difficult for them to understand what goes on in the field:

Marketers are not necessarily formulating strategies based on what actually happens in the sales world. See there are different situations, there are different geographies, there are different customer groups, and marketing is so far removed that many times, they assume that they have a strategy to tackle all of these differences. (Lesley, Sales)

In their opinion, the lack of direct customer contact and inability to monitor competitive activity on a day-to-day basis renders marketers' strategies ineffective. Salespeople further note that they can better understand customer needs and fulfill them since they are in constant contact with customers. Accordingly, salespeople view marketers not as a strategic hub, but purely as a support function. They expect marketers to reach out to the salespeople proactively, serve them as and when they needed help, and take care of the 'little things'. Roger is very emphatic in noting this:

A lot of things that we need from marketing are very basic ... for example, references that the customers may want in our support literature, product brochures, or some scientific data ... maybe some assistance with presenting to our customers and relieving salespeople from all the firefight they might need to engage in on the field so that they can do their job. Marketing's responsibility is really to take care of the little things ... I guess that should be their main role. I think of them as purely a support function ... salespeople are doers. (Roger, Sales)

My sales informants viewed marketers as 'distant and objective' from about customers and market opportunities. They expected marketers to be passionate about 'customer pains', be in direct customer contact, and not stay in their abstract zones. Doing this, they mentioned, may help marketers understand market reality from the salesperson's and customer's point of view:

There is an ivory tower mentality within the marketing group ... they stay distant ... from us, from the customers ... they are not willing to look at the customers from different angles ... only the marketing angle. They do not want to look at the day-to-day, tactical side of business ... and they're missing out on a lot of opportunities. (Mac, Sales)

Last, they expressed frustration over the fact that, many times, marketers hold a lot of control over strategic processes, which makes the salesperson's life difficult. They expected marketers to appreciate the fact that there can be many unknowns in the marketplace and that they are not able to capture what those unknowns could be without stepping out of their offices.

Overall, salespeople's expectations of marketing's role within the strategic process contradict how marketers view their role to be in the organizations. While marketers think of their role as strategic, salespeople view and expect them to act as purely a support function. They believe that marketers are removed from reality and hence cannot understand the pulse of the market appropriately; something that they are able to do owing to their proximity to the customers. Salespeople also expect marketers to be passionate about customers' causes and get involved with them in helping customers out. This contrasts with marketers' unwillingness to get involved in tactical issues such as closing sales or getting too involved with one particular customer.

A summary of the above discussion is offered in Figure 1. The second research question asked how these differences (similarities) in sales and marketing's perceptions of their own and their counterparts' role may create challenges (serve as facilitators) for functional executives as they prepare for the emergence of a strategic sales organization and its related imperatives. The next section highlights the 'role-related' and 'process-related' facilitators and challenges for marketing and sales.

Facilitators for marketers

I found that while marketers did not want to be extensively involved in the tactical aspects of strategy implementation, they were mindful that they are one of the crucial sales support functions within the organization. This coincides with salespeople's expectations that marketing be the support function. This overlap in marketing and sales' thinking can serve as a facilitator for marketers as they prepare to embrace the new paradigm. Specifically, marketers may take specific steps toward integrating their work processes with those of the sales organization so that they are able to work across their traditional boundaries, support sales force, and meet customer requirements. Although my data showed that there were significant differences in each function's perception (and expectation) regarding the nature of support marketing may provide, marketers may build on the fundamental commonality in their thought processes with the sales organization (marketing's role as a support function) and work on their differences to improve strategy creation and implementation activities. This may help them in achieving interfunctional integration wherein marketing's activities are increasingly supportive of the sales organization (Rouziès et al., 2005).

M A R K E T I N G S A Y S	**Our role is strategic; we must** ○ act as a strategic hub -- coordinating among diverse functional units ○ be global, strategic, and long-term in our thinking and actions ○ keep the organization aligned with the market requirements ○ serve as owners and nurturers of brands and value propositions **We are the decision-makers; we should** ○ not be delegating decisions to sales organization ○ be accountable for getting things done ○ be responsible for providing comprehensive customer solution **Sales force depends on us; we must** ○ arm salespeople with information, tools, and talk tracks they need ○ be trainers and coaches for salespeople ○ be able to collect feedback from customers ○ be a medium that carries information back and forth between sales and the rest of the organization **We should not be expected to** ○ make a sale happen ○ be an 'on-call' sales support ○ be a 'super-rep' and go on the field with them to tackle major accounts	**Sales' main task is implementation; they should** ○ be 'on the top of their game' in execution; follow processes meticulously ○ be organized and thoughtful in strategy execution ○ take the lead in implementation ○ follow all instructions; not do things only if there is something in it for them ○ follow suggested processes so that things get done, not devise their own processes **Sales should learn the importance of long-term strategy; they should** ○ act as business managers -- like marketing's extension in the field ○ be long-term relationship builders and focus on long-term growth ○ be experts on their customers, and build and own customer relationships ○ be proactive; not reactive **Sales should be cooperative; they should** ○ not be territorial and treat marketers' attempts to interact with customers as intrusion ○ not create boundaries around customers ○ use their connections with other salespeople to strengthen strategy implementation and improve work processes; not derail strategies
S A L E S S A Y S	**Our role within the firm is very strategic since we** ○ are passionate champions of customers' causes ○ look for opportunities to develop or cement customer relationships ○ collect verbal and nonverbal cues from customers ○ stay hungry for knowledge and possess tacit customer knowledge **We cannot** ○ be expected to move our focus away from immediate goals to purely long-term objectives ○ be asked to sacrifice products when marketing thinks it no longer makes sense **It is difficult for us to** ○ remain disciplined within the boundaries of the prescribed processes ○ always keep the bigger strategic picture in mind	**Marketing is purely a support function; they should** ○ serve as an 'on-call' sales support system ○ take care of the 'little things' as and when salespeople would demand it ○ proactively reach out to salespeople ○ interact with customers in their presence; not by-pass them **Marketing should develop a sense of reality; they should** ○ not always remain in an abstract zone ○ not stay distant, rational, and non-passionate; they should be as involved with customers as we are ○ not hold so much control over strategic tasks that salespeople's work depends on marketing's timely cooperation ○ be aware that there can be many 'unknowns' in the market that they cannot anticipate sitting in their offices while strategizing **Given the luxury of time they have, marketers should** ○ be long-range strategic thinkers

Figure 1. How sales and marketing view themselves and the other function.

From a process standpoint, marketing's willingness to act as a sales force liaison and help salespeople navigate the organizational bureaucracy so that the firm may provide a timely, value added customer solution, can serve as an important facilitating factor.

Strategic sales organization requires that the intelligence developed by the sales force be utilized in strategy creation. If marketers are able to serve as a liaison, channel information collected by the salespeople back into the organization, and coordinate activities among the various departments such as R&D, accounting, pricing, and so on, firms are able to act on the intelligence and respond to market needs. This is consistent with the thesis on market orientation, which requires different organizational functions to collectively respond to market realities (Kohli & Jaworski, 1990).

Challenges for marketers

The perception disparities discussed earlier may create important challenges for marketers as they work toward adopting the strategic sales organization paradigm. First, this paradigm argues for the sales force's extensive involvement in strategy creation and customer portfolio decision making. Consistently, marketers may have a difficult time in delegating the decision-making authority to the sales organization. They will also face challenges in altering their involvement in the strategic decision-making process and giving up 'control' of the many activities such as segmentation, communication, and product positioning that they are traditionally involved in.

Second, in order to effectively deal with the strategic sales organization, marketers will have to develop a stronger customer focus – both on internal (salespeople) and external customers. This may prove to be a challenge since they will have to rethink their strategy-making processes so that they are able to incorporate salespeople's perspective in marketing strategies. They may also need to create new work processes to facilitate easy integration of salespeople's points of view. Marketers' inability in addressing these issues will jeopardize the firm's efforts to integrate the two departments and the organization may risk losing the critical intelligence generated by the field force.

Third, owing to the physical distance between them and final customers, marketers may find it difficult to remain closer to them. If marketers were to succeed in this endeavor, they will have to be passionate about customers and get involved in working alongside the sales force on customer-related issues on a regular basis; something that they are not very excited about.

Last, marketers may find it challenging to build a bridge between their strategic thinking with the micro-level focus of salespeople. Similarly, they may find it challenging to help salespeople connect their micro-level, tactical focus with the bigger picture. This *disconnect* between the two functions may hamper the processes of integration and involvement.

Facilitators for sales executives

My data suggested that both marketing and salespeople expect the sales organization to act as the 'voice of the customer' and serve as 'customer advocate' within the firm. This indicates a consensus between these functions about the importance of salespeople in bringing customer intelligence within the organization. This can thus facilitate the process of integrating the market intelligence that the salespeople may bring in, and also involving them within the strategy-making process, thereby ensuring that marketing strategies are customer-focused, and that the firm is market-oriented.

From a process point of view, marketers expect salespeople to develop customer relationships. This is consistent with salespeople's perspective that one of their key competencies is connecting with their customers and relationship building. Salespeople may build on this conceptual overlap to exhibit how they may leverage these relationships to generate superior customer intelligence.

Challenges for sales executives

My data brought forth a few challenges that the sales executives will need to overcome as they prepare to be a part of the strategic sales organization. The first challenge is that salespeople will have to develop a business mindset and blend their 'short-term, selling orientation' with a broader strategic perspective. This change in salespeople's perspective is crucial, because it will allow for the sales force to alter its activities so that they are consistent with the prescribed marketing strategies. This may also facilitate the process of sales–marketing integration through joint activities. Further, once the sales organization adapts this approach, the intelligence developed by salespeople will be more aligned with what marketing expects it to bring in.

From a process standpoint, my data suggest that the sales organizations will encounter four challenges. First, similar to marketers, salespeople will find it challenging to bridge the gap between their own perspectives of the market and the broader organizational strategies. Second, marketers' insistence that salespeople use a structured, methodical approach when it comes to implementing marketing strategy can prove to be a challenge. They will have to internalize and adopt a structured approach to strategy implementation, and also generate appropriate intelligence that can be transferred back to marketing. If salespeople do not follow a structured approach, it can create process-integration challenges for marketers. Third, salespeople may find it hard to let go of the control over their customers and provide marketers with easy access to their customers. Last, they may need to rethink how they may utilize the informal sales networks to the benefits of their marketing strategies.

A brief summary of the above discussion is provided in Figure 2.

Discussion

Using qualitative data collected from sales and marketing executives, this study highlighted the similarities and differences between sales and marketing executives' perceptions of their and their counterparts' roles within the strategy-making process. Further, it built on these insights to highlight factors that may facilitate and challenge a marketer or a salesperson as he/she prepares to embrace the new strategic sales organization. In this section, I highlight the theoretical contributions of this study. It is followed by a discussion of its managerial implications, limitations, and suggestions for future research.

Contributions

This paper makes four contributions to marketing literature. First, while the marketing–sales interface literature has highlighted the acrimonious relationship between the two functions (Dewsnap & Jobber, 2000; Rouziès et al., 2005), research to date has not specifically explored the nuances of each function's expectations regarding their own and their counterparts' roles within the strategy-making process. This study provides a detailed comparison of the role expectations across this interface that highlights a stark contrast between how marketing and sales personnel view themselves and how they are viewed by their counterparts. While the extant literature highlights the differences in cultures,

Facilitators and challengers for marketers:		
	Facilitators	**Challenges**
Role/ mind-set	o Marketing as a support system	o Delegation of authority o Internal customer focus o Customer passion and interaction o Bridging long-term strategic focus with short-term tactical elements
Process	o Liaison for sales force	o Willingness and ability to bridge macro perspective with micro-level tactics o Tactical involvement
Facilitators and challengers for salespeople:		
	Facilitators	**Challenges**
Role/ mind-set	o Voice of the customer/customer advocate	o Selling vs. business management
Process	o Relationship building	o Willingness and ability to bridge micro-level tactical issues with the global, strategic issues o Methodical approach to strategy implementation o Dissolving customer boundaries o Use of social networks within sales organization

Figure 2. Embracing the new paradigm.

thought worlds, and strategic/tactical foci of sales and marketing (Homburg et al., 2008), this is the first study that I am aware of that brings forth the nuances of role expectations within this interface.

Second, while scholars have started acknowledging the changing nature of sales organization (Ingram, 2004; Leigh & Marshall, 2001), specific guidance regarding what the emergence of a strategic sales organization entails for sales and marketing functions is not offered in the literature to date. While Piercy (2006) has noted that one must pay attention to the marketing–sales interface while studying strategic sales organizational imperatives, this is the first empirical study to integrate the interface dynamics with this new paradigmatic thinking. In integrating these two streams of literatures, this study thus situates the emergent phenomenon of strategic sales organization within the context of our extant knowledge and provides a comprehensive thesis about what this transformation means for the sales–marketing interface.

Third, this study builds on the strategic imperatives proposed by Piercy (2006) to highlight a set of facilitators and challenges that sales and marketing managers may encounter as they prepare for this paradigm shift. Interestingly, these role-related and process-related challenges and facilitators to the strategic imperatives emanate from the similarities and differences in the role expectations within this interface. Together, this collective framework embodying the analysis of role expectations and the resultant challenges/facilitators for strategic imperatives constitutes an important step in understanding the implications of this new paradigm on interfunctional dynamics.

Managerial implications

Managers may find the insights from this study useful. First, both marketing and sales professionals will find the comparison between how they view themselves and the other function, and how the other function views itself and them enlightening. This may require them to periodically check-in with their counterparts and assess the extent of overlap and disparity between their perceptions of self and the other function. Doing so may help them reduce potential challenges as they prepare for the new strategic sales organization and its related imperatives.

Findings of this study indicate that sales professionals must remain aware of how the many challenges these differences bring forth affect the firm's strategy-making and execution processes. They will need to adopt a business manager's mindset and evaluate how their tactical field activities affect broader parameters such as business profitability, market share, and long-term growth of the brands. Accordingly, they may need to make modifications in their day-to-day sales processes so that they do not compromise the firm's long-term goals. For this to become reality, salespeople will need to think beyond their own territories, and also accept the fact that the global/national picture may have things that they may not have seen in their own territories. Salespeople may also find it useful to bridge the micro-processes and goals they set for themselves with the broader strategic processes that marketing may initiate. This may be achieved using a methodical approach to developing an execution plan and may lead to better integration between sales and marketing's work processes. Further, my findings indicate that in order to enhance the quality of market intelligence, salespeople will have to desist from erecting 'boundaries' around their customers and preventing marketers from getting direct access to those customers. Doing so may facilitate the process of integration between sales and marketing. As noted earlier, there exist many informal networks within sales organizations wherein salespeople from different territories connect with one another to exchange critical market information. My findings suggest that these networks can be put to good use so that they facilitate cross-pollination of ideas and best practices across different sales territories thereby leading to enhanced sales effectiveness. Salespeople may also build on the commonalities in their thinking with marketers and make the firms customer-oriented by acting as customer advocates. Last, they can build strong customer relationships and create competitive barriers.

Marketing professionals may use the findings of this study as well. Specifically, this study will highlight the need for them to internalize the fact that involving the sales force in the strategic decision-making process, and allowing them to take some decisions regarding their key customers on their own does not constitute loss of authority. Further, marketers will need to view firm performance as a shared responsibility, and treat their sales colleagues as strategic partners who can make informed decisions. Marketers will have to be more aligned with the needs of the sales force and insure that the solutions they create are comprehensive for internal customers as well. Specifically, they will need to make sure that prior to creating marketing strategies, salespeople's perspectives have been heard and their ideas have been incorporated in the marketing strategies. With respect to external customers, marketers must make attempts to be closer to their final customers. This may be done by involving themselves with specific key accounts, and closely working with the sales force to make sure that the account is served appropriately. Last, as the firm moves toward the strategic sales organization paradigm, it might become imperative for marketers to bridge the gap between the macro-level strategies that they are conversant with, and the micro-level tactics that salespeople think in terms of.

Marketers may build on the commonality between their thought process with the sales organization and institute processes so that they act as a liaison for the sales force. Further, they may constantly look for ways to support the sales organization, and accommodate them in times of urgency.

Limitations and future research directions

Before I conclude, I wish to note two limitations of this study. First, the nuances of the role identified here, by no means constitute an exhaustive list. This is an exploratory study and there may be a bigger repertoire of nuances that may affect the strategy-making and implementation process than I have identified here. Further, owing to the multidimensional nature and complexity of the phenomenon, it is also likely that multiple nuances I identify across the various dimensions may interact and have differential effects on strategy implementation processes. Second, the data for this study came only from participant interviews. I believe that if I spent time within informant organizations and worked with sales/marketing professionals, deeper insights into this phenomenon might have emerged.

The findings of this study can serve as a foundation for future research in this area. Future research may investigate additional nuances of role expectations than those I have identified herein. It will be interesting to explore additional areas where sales and marketing may hold similar and different opinions of themselves and their counterparts. Relatedly, there is likely to be a bigger inventory of challenges and facilitating factors than I have identified in this paper. Scholars may explore these as well. This is a qualitative study, the findings of which may be subjected to a quantitative analysis in future research.

Acknowledgements

The author wishes to acknowledge two grants for providing support for this research: Research Assistance Grant from the Faculty Development Center, and Dean's Summer Research Grant from the Opus College of Business; both at the University of St Thomas.

References

Beverland, M., Steel, M., & Dapiran, G.P. (2006). Cultural frames that drive sales and marketing apart: An exploratory study. *Journal of Business & Industrial Marketing, 21,* 386–394.

Carpenter, P. (1992). Bridging the gap between marketing and sales. *Sales and Marketing Management,* 29–31.

Cespedes, F.V. (1993). Coordinating sales and marketing in consumer goods firm. *Journal of Consumer Marketing, 10,* 37–55.

Cespedes, F.V. (1996). Beyond teamwork: How the wise can synchronize. *Marketing Management, 5*(Spring), 24–37.

Challey Group. (1998). *The customer-selected world class sales excellence research report.* Dayton, OH: The H.R. Challey Group.

Colletti, J.A., & Chonko, L.B. (1997). Change management initiatives: Moving sales organizations from obsolescence to high performance. *Journal of Personal Selling & Sales Management, 17*(Spring), 1–30.

Corley, K.G., & Gioia, D.A. (2004). Identity ambiguity and change in the wake of a corporate spin-off. *Administrative Science Quarterly, 29,* 173–208.

Creswell, J.W. (2007). *Qualitative inquiry & research design* (2nd ed.). Thousand Oaks, CA: Sage Publications.

Dawes, P.L., & Massey, G.R. (2005). Antecedents of conflict in marketing's cross-functional relationship with sales. *European Journal of Marketing, 39,* 1327–1344.

Deshpande, R. (1983). 'Paradigms lost': On theory and method in research in marketing. *Journal of Marketing, 47*(Fall), 101–110.

Dewsnap, B., & Jobber, D. (2000). The sales–marketing interface in consumer packaged-goods companies: A conceptual framework. *Journal of Personal Selling & Sales Management*, *20*(Spring), 109–119.

Dewsnap, B., & Jobber, D. (2002). A social psychological model of relations between marketing and sales. *European Journal of Marketing*, *36*, 874–894.

Flint, D.J., Woodruff, R.B., & Gardial, S.F. (2002). Exploring the phenomenon of customers' desired value change in a business-to-business context. *Journal of Marketing*, *66*(10), 102–117.

Guenzi, P., & Troilo, G. (2006). Developing marketing capabilities for customer value creation through marketing–sales integration. *Industrial Marketing Management*, *35*(11), 974–988.

Guenzi, P., & Troilo, G. (2007). The joint contribution of marketing and sales to the creation of superior customer value. *Journal of Business Research*, *60*(2), 98–107.

Gummesson, E. (2003). All research is interpretive! *Journal of Business & Industrial Marketing*, *18*, 482–492.

Homburg, C., & Jensen, O. (2007). The thought worlds of marketing and sales: Which differences make a difference? *Journal of Marketing*, *71*(July), 124–142.

Homburg, C., Ove, J., & Krohmer, H. (2008). Configurations of marketing and sales: A taxonomy. *Journal of Marketing*, *72*(March), 133–154.

Hutt, M.D. (1995). Cross-functional working relationships in marketing. *Journal of the Academy of Marketing Science*, *23*(Fall), 351–357.

Ingram, T.N. (2004). Future themes in sales and sales management: Complexity, collaboration, and accountability. *Journal of Marketing Theory & Practice*, *12*(Fall), 18–28.

Ingram, T.N., LaForge, R.W., & Leigh, T.W. (2002). Selling in the new millennium: A joint agenda. *Industrial Marketing Management*, *31*(7), 559–567.

Kohli, A.K., & Jaworski, B.J. (1990). Market orientation: The construct, research propositions, and managerial implications. *Journal of Marketing*, *54*(4), 1–18.

Kotler, P., Rackham, N., & Krishnaswamy, S. (2006). Ending the war between sales and marketing. *Harvard Business Review*, *84*, 68–78.

Leigh, T.W., & Marshall, G.W. (2001). Research priorities in sales strategy and performance. *Journal of Personal Selling and Sales Management*, *XXI*(2), 83–93.

Le Meunier-FitzHugh, K., & Piercy, N.F. (2006). Integrating marketing intelligence sources. *International Journal of Market Research*, *48*, 699–716.

Le Meunier-FitzHugh, K., & Piercy, N.F. (2007). Does collaboration between sales and marketing affect business performance? *Journal of Personal Selling & Sales Management*, *27*(Summer), 207–220.

Lincoln, Y.S., & Guba, E.G. (1985). *Naturalistic inquiry*. Beverly Hills, CA: Sage Publications.

Lorge, S. (1999). Marketers are from Mars, salespeople from Venus. *Sales and Marketing Management*, *151*(4), 26–33.

Matthyssens, P., & Johnston, W.J. (2006). Marketing and sales: Optimization of a neglected relationship. *Journal of Business & Industrial Marketing*, *21*, 338–345.

McCracken, G. (1988). *The long interview*. Newbury Park, CA: Sage Publications.

Noble, C.H., & Mokwa, M.P. (1999). Implementing marketing strategies: Developing and testing a managerial theory. *Journal of Marketing*, *63*(4), 57–73.

Piercy, N.F. (2006). The strategic sales organization. *Marketing Review*, *6*(Spring), 3–28.

Piercy, N.F., & Lane, N. (2003). Transformation of the traditional salesforce: Imperatives for intelligence, interface and integration. *Journal of Marketing Management*, *19*(7), 563–582.

Rouziès, D., Anderson, E., Kohli, A.K., Michaels, R.E., Weitz, B.A., & Zoltners, A.A. (2005). Sales and marketing integration: A proposed framework. *Journal of Personal Selling & Sales Management*, *25*(Spring), 113–122.

Rust, R.T., & Cooil, B. (1994). Reliability measures for qualitative data: Theory and implications. *Journal of Marketing Research*, *31*(1), 1–14.

Strahle, W.M., Spiro, R.L., & Acito, F. (1996). Marketing and sales: Strategic alignment and functional implementation. *Journal of Personal Selling & Sales Management*, *16*(Winter), 1–20.

Strauss, A., & Corbin, J. (1990). *Basics of qualitative research*. Newbury Park, CA: Sage.

Strauss, A.L., & Corbin, J. (1998). *Basics of qualitative research: Grounded theory procedures and techniques*. Newbury Park, CA: Sage Publications.

Tuli, K.R., Kohli, A.K., & Bharadwaj, S.G. (2007). Rethinking customer solutions: From product bundles to relational processes. *Journal of Marketing*, *71*(7), 1–17.

Webster, F.E., & Montgomery, D.B. (1997). Marketing's interfunctional interfaces: The MSI workshop on management of corporate fault zones. *Journal of Market Focused Management*, 2(1), 7–26.

Appendix 1. Interview protocol

(1) What do you see as the role of the sales organization in your firm's strategic activities?

(2) What do you see as the role of the marketing organization in your firm's strategic activities?

(3) Have you observed any changes in the roles and responsibilities of the sales organization in your firm's strategic process? Please elaborate.

(4) Do you foresee any change in the sales organization's role in your firm's strategic activities in near future? Why? Why not?

(5) What specific changes do you anticipate to happen in your sales organization's role in the near future?

(6) Have you observed any changes in the roles and responsibilities of the marketing organization in your firm's strategic process? Please elaborate.

(7) Do you foresee any change in the marketing organization's role in your firm's strategic activities in near future? Why? Why not?

(8) What specific changes do you anticipate to happen in your marketing organization's role in near future?

Collaboration between sales and marketing, market orientation and business performance in business-to-business organisations

Kenneth Le Meunier-FitzHugh and Nikala Lane

The study considers whether improving collaboration between sales and marketing may provide benefits to organisations through greater market orientation and improved business performance. The influence of market intelligence systems and management attitudes towards coordination on market orientation and collaboration between sales and marketing are also explored. The study was carried out through a survey of senior executives in large, UK, business-to-business organisations from a number of industries and the results indicate that there is an interrelationship between market intelligence systems, management attitude towards coordination, and collaboration between sales and marketing. The results also confirm that collaboration between sales and marketing has a positive and significant impact on both market orientation and business performance.

This paper will consider the inter-relationship between the sales and marketing interface and market orientation in large, business-to-business (B2B) organisations in the UK market. Although it is widely accepted that the internal coordination of functions is essential to creating a market orientation approach (e.g. Kohli & Jaworski, 1990; Slater & Narver, 1994), the interface between two essential functions to business success, sales and marketing, has been under-researched. Further, there is evidence to indicate that this relationship exhibits lack of cohesion, distrust, and even conflict (e.g. Dewsnap & Jobber, 2000; Kotler, Rackham, & Krishnaswamy, 2006; Rouzies et al., 2005). It has been suggested that some of the divisions between sales and marketing have been created by fundamental job differences and different thought worlds (Donath, 2004; Homburg & Jensen, 2007). Further, Corstjens and Corstjens (1999) indicate that a lack of cooperation between sales and marketing has the potential to damage the overall success of the organisation. More critically the importance of collaborative sales and marketing functions has been overlooked in its contribution, not only to market orientation, but also to improved business performance.

It may be argued that sales and marketing functions play a crucial role in the creation of market orientation as they are customer facing and boundary spanning, so they are visible to the customer. This interface also impacts upon the effectiveness of other functions within the organisation through interactions with customers and market sensing activities (e.g. Narver & Slater, 1990). It is therefore suggested that two other factors, market intelligence systems and management attitudes towards coordination, have some impact on collaboration between sales and marketing and on market orientation. This paper will aim to establish the critical importance of a collaborative relationship between sales and marketing to, and its impact upon, market orientation and business performance.

Market orientation has been defined as referring to the 'generation, dissemination, and responsiveness to market intelligence by organizations' (Tadepalli & Avila, 1999, p. 69), and therefore an important element in the creation of a market orientation is an effective market intelligence system. Market intelligence consists of three elements: collection; storage/analysis; and dissemination. For an intelligence system to be effective all three elements should work in concert (Le Meunier-FitzHugh & Piercy, 2006). In addition, there is evidence to show that an effective marketing intelligence process should include data from a number of sources, including the sales force, and that the information derived from the system should be fed back to these sources (Evans & Schlacter, 1985). The market intelligence system thereby provides an opportunity for sales and marketing to collaborate on an area that is relevant and beneficial to both parties. It follows therefore that there should be a positive relationship between an effective market intelligence system and the level of collaboration between sales and marketing, as well as between an effective marketing intelligence process and market orientation.

Finally the concept of market orientation has been seen as 'a cornerstone of both strategic marketing and strategic management' (Harris & Ogbonna, 2000, p. 318), and may be related to the required levels of organisational coordination and responsiveness to the market needs and competitor's activities (Kohli & Jaworski, 1990; Narver & Slater, 1990; Siguaw, Brown, & Widing, 1994). Both of these concepts require senior managers to provide strategic direction, and to align goals and activities. It is proposed that a positive senior management attitude towards coordination is essential both to establishing effective collaboration between sales and marketing and the creation of market orientation.

There is considerable evidence to indicate that market orientation has a direct impact on business performance (Pulendran, Speed, & Widing, 2003; Slater & Narver, 2000), but the contribution of this paper will be to explore how sales and marketing collaboration impacts on market orientation, management attitudes towards coordination, and market intelligence systems, thereby adding to the scant literature on the sales and marketing interface and considering its impact on business performance. This paper will explore these themes through a survey of senior managers with the aim of providing insight into the relationship between sales and marketing, market orientation, and their impact on business performance.

Conceptual development

The conceptual development considers the interrelationship between the four elements identified in contributing to business performance (see Figure 1). These four elements include market intelligence, management attitudes towards coordination, collaboration between sales and marketing, and marketing orientation.

Market orientation and business performance

Kohli and Jaworski (1990) suggest that market orientated organisations are more closely aligned to customer needs and are more in tune with the marketplace and have greater

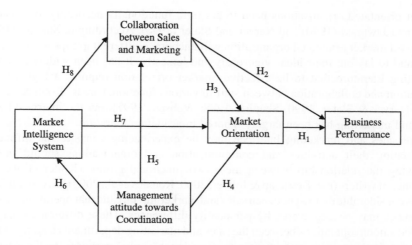

Figure 1. Exploring the relationship between collaboration between sales and marketing, market orientation and business performance.

internal coordination providing increased flexibility in response than organisations that are not market orientated and that this will lead to an improvement in overall improvement in sales, market share and profits. This proposition was supported by Slater and Narver (2000) who found that superior business performance was associated with a market orientation and this result was robust across industry boundaries. Market orientation should be seen as an organisation-wide activity that relates directly to the performance of the organisation rather than a single functional activity according to Webster (1988), but Doyle (2002, p. 48) warned that organisations should not 'make the mistake of thinking that becoming marketing orientated means making the marketing department the primary function of the business'. It is more important that the organisation is 'structured around major customers and markets, not products, and will integrate sales, product strategy, distribution, and marketing communications competences and activities' (Webster, 1997, p. 64). Research by Morgan and Turnell (2003) also found that a market orientation is positively related to improved market performance. There is therefore considerable academic support for the first hypothesis:

H1: Market orientation is positively associated with improved business performance.

Collaboration between sales and marketing, market orientation and business performance

The concept of collaboration between sales and marketing does not require that the two groups are merged or that their activities are integrated into a single function. Rather it refers to the ability of two separate, functional groups to coordinate their activities, communicate across boundaries, and create a team spirit and common goals (Khan, 1996). We believe collaboration between sales and marketing will allow them to work together effectively, presenting a coherent message to the marketplace and sharing decisions and objectives. Functional teams that stress collaboration in performing their activities and in making decisions are less likely to be working at cross purposes (Hult, Ketchen, & Slater, 2002). To align activities, collaboration cannot just be based on close working relationships, but must be supported by aligned goals and integrative processes.

Market orientated organisations need to act intra-functionally according to research by Kohli and Jaworski (1990) and Narver and Slater (1990). According to Shapiro (1988), a successful market orientated organisation will encourage different groups to listen to each other and to lay out their ideas vigorously and honestly. It has been widely accepted in marketing literature that to be effective, market orientation requires a high degree of integration and collaboration between staff in various functional areas (Kohli & Jaworski, 1990; Narver & Slater, 1990; Shapiro, 1988; Webster, 1997), but the interface between sales and marketing has been largely ignored in academic literature.

The sales and marketing interface may be experiencing considerable difficulty in coordinating their activities and communication and organisations should invest in improving the relationship between these two functional groups (Kotler et al., 2006). A number of writers (e.g. Dewsnap & Jobber, 2000; Rouzies et al., 2005) have identified that there is considerable distrust between sales and marketing staff and that operational and goal differences may be aggravated by personality differences. These differences may have impeded smooth operations between the sales and marketing departments leading to lack of coherence in communication messages, working at cross purposes and occasionally obstructive behaviour (Kotler et al., 2006). The suggestion is that sales and marketing are areas that are customer facing and that any lack of consistency in performance will be noticed by customers and this may adversely affect the organisation's market orientation. The reverse of this contention is that that improved collaboration between sales and marketing will have a positive and significant impact upon market orientation.

The concept that there may be a positive link between improved internal collaboration and business performance has been suggested by a number of writers (e.g. Kohli & Jaworski, 1990; Morgan & Turnell, 2003; Narver & Slater, 1990; Ruekert & Walker, 1987). It would appear to be logical to propose that improvements in collaboration between sales and marketing (who are often viewed externally as a single function by customers (Schmonsees, 2006)) would have a significant and direct impact on business performance. Certainly, Corstjens and Corstjens (1999) indicated that a lack of cooperation between sales and marketing has the potential to damage the overall success of the organisation. In addition two areas that are directly affected by sales and marketing activities, a customer orientation and competitor orientation, are both positively related to improving market orientation (Morgan & Turnell, 2003). Therefore, it is proposed that improvements in collaboration between sales and marketing will positively influence both market orientation and business performance and the hypotheses will be:

H2: Collaboration between sales and marketing functions is positively associated with business performance.

H3: Collaboration between sales and marketing functions is positively associated with market orientation.

Management attitudes towards coordination

Senior managers have the capability to encourage departmental staff to achieve mutual understanding, share resources and vision, achieve mutual goals and work informally together (Khan, 1996). The concept that a management attitude to improving processes is an essential element to improving internal processes has been confirmed by a number of studies. Further, through leadership and staff empowerment, senior management are responsible for establishing the culture of the organisation, enabling them to create and execute strategies to achieve objectives (Jaworski & Kohli, 1993; Slater & Narver, 1994).

Creating a market orientation driven from senior management is a philosophy adopted by the whole organisation, not simply a marketing focus (Doyle, 2002). If marketing activities are given an unnecessary importance within the organisation inter-functional conflict may be aggravated (Slater & Narver, 1994). Interdepartmental conflict may reduce market orientation, and for market orientation to be effective, it must be the driving force of the organisation and this can only be initiated by senior managers (Jaworski & Kohli, 1993).

There is little doubt that senior managers have the capability to create collaboration between sales and marketing, but they have to appreciate the importance of investing time and energy in achieving this objective. The objective should be to create an *esprit de corps* between sales and management through the discussion of strategy for cross-functional responsibilities and communication of common aims (Slater & Narver, 1994). One of the barriers to creating collaboration between sales and marketing may be differences between marketing having a longer-term perspective and the more immediate targeted concerns of sales. Assessing the trade-offs between short-term financial performance and the future, long-term financial performance may be difficult for many senior managers (Webster, 1988, 1997) and Simkin (2002) noted that a lack of senior management support for collaboration is frequently a major barrier to integration. Therefore, it is the attitude of senior managers to creating coordination between functions that is crucial to establishing collaboration between sales and marketing.

Senior management support for the creation of an effective market intelligence system is also essential. Senior managers are able to facilitate the creation of information systems that cross functional boundaries and which will allow market information to be more effective, as it has been gathered from a number of sources (marketing and sales). Market intelligence must also be widely disseminated in good time to provide maximum benefit (Le Meunier-FitzHugh & Piercy, 2006). The development and communication of good market intelligence throughout the organisations is likely to lead to improved customer focus and therefore improved business performance. Therefore the hypotheses will be:

H4: A proactive management attitude towards coordination between sales and marketing is positively associated with market orientation.

H5: A proactive management attitude towards coordination between sales and marketing is positively associated with collaboration between sales and marketing.

H6: A proactive management attitude towards coordination between sales and marketing is positively associated with an effective market intelligence system.

Market intelligence system

For the market intelligence system to be effective in contributing to collaboration between sales and marketing, both parties are required to be involved in the process. It appears from previous research that using the sales force to collect information about the marketplace is legitimate and efficient (Grove, Carlson, & Dorsch, 1992), and that many organisations follow this approach, but it has been noted that salespeople may be reluctant to pass information on to marketing if there is no clear benefit in so doing (Homburg, Workman, & Jensen, 2000). If sales people are actively encouraged to participate in market intelligence systems, it provides a forum through which sales can communicate with marketing. Shared information about customer needs and assessing new market segments should include up-to-date intelligence on competitors' capabilities, products and services that may be most effectively provided by the sales force (e.g. Cross, Hartley, Rudelius, & Vassey, 2001). However, it is important to note that the market information should be processed and disseminated back to sales and marketing staff within a short time-frame to be most effective (Grove et al., 1992). Therefore, an integrative market intelligence system will provide a process where sales and marketing can collaborate to their mutual benefit.

Jaworski and Kohli (1993) identified that market orientated organisations rely on the organisation-wide generation of market intelligence and the dissemination of that intelligence across all departments. Evans and Schlacter (1985) found that market information may be collected and available in many organisations, but their processes and structures may fail to analyse and disseminate the information adequately. Market orientation requires 'that all information on all important buying influences permeates every corporate function and that strategic and tactical decisions are made interfunctionally and interdivisionally' (Reid, Luxton, & Mavondo, 2005, p. 15). It is suggested that this may not be occurring between sales and marketing functions. Effective interdepartmental communication will be part of effective collaboration and has been linked to a number of positive outcomes including improved market orientation (Kohli & Jaworski, 1990). An organisation's competitive advantage is increasingly reliant on their ability to use market intelligence effectively (Maltz & Kohli, 2000). Therefore, it is proposed that market orientation and collaboration between sales and marketing will be facilitated through market intelligence systems. Consequently, the hypotheses will be:

H7: An effective market intelligence system is positively associated with collaboration between sales and marketing.

H8: An effective market intelligence system is positively associated with market orientation.

Methodology

The conceptual framework was developed through exploratory interviews with practitioners to aid the development of the questionnaire. Nine semi-structured interviews were carried out with senior members of staff in three contrasting organisations; a publisher, consumer goods manufacturer, and industrial goods manufacturer. Interviews took place with the head of sales, head of marketing, and their line manager (who were all members of the senior management team). Following this exploratory research, a questionnaire was developed and mailed survey was undertaken with senior executives of large, UK business-to-business (B2B) organisations. Large organisations have been defined as any company whose turnover exceeds £11.2 million (*Small and medium enterprise definitions*, 2004).

Sample selection

One thousand randomly selected wholesalers, industrial goods manufacturers, consumer goods manufacturers and publishers were selected from a list provided by a commercial agency. The multi-page questionnaire was mailed to Managing Directors/Chief Executives of each organisation with a covering letter. A reminder letter was sent approximately two weeks after the initial letter and then a second copy of the questionnaire with covering letter was sent approximately two weeks after the reminder letter. Finally, a letter was sent approximately six weeks after the initial contact. The letters were sent on university headed paper as recommended by Houston and Nevin (1977), and the participants were offered a summary copy of the results of the survey. No other incentives were offered.

Table 1. Survey response rates.

Sample size	Total 1000
Total number of respondents	223
Total number of usable respondents	**146**
Turnover too low (less than £11m)	24
No sales or marketing dept	10
Do not do surveys	13
No longer trading	25
Unusable	5
Total number ineligible respondents	**77**
Response rate	**14.6%**

Response rate

In total the survey generated 223 (22.3%) responses, of which 77 were unusable (see Table 1). The 14.6% useable responses were within the expected response rate for surveys directed to Managing Directors/Chief Executives (Menon, Bharadwaj, & Howell, 1996; Slotegraaf & Dickson, 2004). Although the questionnaire was addressed to the Managing Director/Chief Executive by name the majority (83.6%) were completed by Senior Managers (Directors), of which 70.5% were Chairman, Chief Executive Officers, Managing Directors, Directors, or General Managers (see Table 2 for the composition of the responses). A MANOVA test was carried out to assess if there was any significant difference between responses by job titles and no significant differences were found.

All organisations were categorised as large UK organisations, but the turnover figures varied providing three groups: those with a turnover between £11 and £20 million (52%); those with a turnover between £21 and 50 million (27%); and those with a turnover of more than £50 million (21%). The responses were also divided into three types of organisation: industrial manufacturers (42%); consumer goods manufacturers (28%); and wholesalers (30%). The findings from each of these groups were tested with a MANOVA test, but no differences were detected between groups.

Two possible sources of sampling error were tested for, non-response error and non-coverage error. Multiple t-tests were performed on the early and late responses to test for non-response bias (Armstrong & Overton, 1977), following the assumption that late respondents are more similar to non-respondents than to the early respondents. With the exception of business performance, the multiple t-tests yielded no significant difference between the two groups at the conventional levels ($p > .05$). The early responses had a significantly higher mean than late responses for the business performance construct,

Table 2. Response sample composition ($N = 146$).

	%
Chairman/CEO/MD/Directors/General Managers	70.5
Marketing Directors /Managers/Executives	11.6
Sales and Marketing Directors/Managers	6.9
Sales Directors/Managers	4.8
Business Development Managers	2.7
Other HR Managers/Accountants/Customer Liaison Managers	3.4
Total number of Senior Managers (Directors)	**83.6**

but we believe that this difference may occur because the less efficient/successful organisations are more likely to respond after being prompted. Nonetheless, it remains a limitation of the research that the sample may be biased towards higher performing companies. The non-coverage error was examined by comparing the characteristics of the respondents (industry type, number of employees, and turnover) with a sample of organisations randomly selected from the non-respondents and again no significant differences were found between the two groups.

Construct operationalisation

The questionnaire was developed from themes and patterns extracted from the exploratory research and extant literature (Churchill & Iacobucci, 2002). These themes were placed in a logical order and, as recommended by Churchill and Iacobucci (2002) and Robinson, Shaver, and Wrightsman (1991), and the majority of the questions were selected from indicators and measures that had been previously developed, tested, and published in other research papers (e.g. Evans & Schlacter, 1985; Hult et al., 2002). This practice also assists with the concurrent validity of the questionnaire. An existing scale could not be found for management attitudes towards coordination, so new questions were developed for this area.

To develop new measures it is essential to ensure that they should reflect the concepts they are trying to measure and that they have face validity (Bryman, 2001). Content validity may be measured through testing new measures with specialists in the area (Moser & Kalton, 1971). Therefore, the initial questionnaire was given to 25 part-time MBA students to review and assess. MBA students were selected because they all are currently working in senior management roles and would be able to comment on how the measures may be received. The effectiveness of the new measures was discussed in detail with a small group selected from these MBA students. This initial development of the questionnaire led to three questions being reworded to improve their clarity. The whole questionnaire was then pre-tested by being sent to 30 Managing Directors from a selected list. There were 20 responses from the pre-test, which resulted in further adjustments. Finally, four marketing academics independently reviewed the questionnaire, but reported that no other changes were necessary. Appendix 1 shows the scale items and the sources for these measures.

Data analysis

The constructs were measured through multiple-item scales and were tested for reliability. The coefficient alphas (see Table 3), the construct means, standard deviations, and inter-correlations are all reported. The Cronbach alpha had a range of .78 to .86, which is satisfactory. Least square regression analysis was employed to evaluate the relationships hypothesised between the antecedent constructs and the dependent variables. Multicollinearity was tested for and was found not to be present, as the variance inflation factors were all below the cut-off value of 10 and all condition indices were well below the critical value of 30.

Findings

Descriptive findings

The descriptive findings provide an overview of the quantitative research. The standard deviation has been used to describe the variants in the data set from the mean. Table 3

Table 3.   Correlation matrix, cronbach alpha, mean and standard deviation.

	Cronbach alpha	Mean (standard deviation)	V1	V2	V3	V4	V5
Management attitudes towards coordination (V1)	0.85	4.91 (1.37)					
Market intelligence system (V2)	0.84	4.60 (1.11)	.499**				
Collaboration between sales and marketing (V3)	0.78	5.31 (1.21)	.599**	.581**			
Market orientation (V4)	0.84	5.14 (0.74)	.523**	.631**	.561**		
Business performance (V5)	0.86	4.66 (1.08)	.336**	.392**	.467**	.504**	

**Correlation is significant at the .001 level (2-tailed).
$N = 146$.

shows that the standard deviation of each item varies from .74 to 1.37, which indicates that the responses are closely aligned to the mean. Management attitudes towards coordination considers the role that senior management plays in coordinating sales and marketing activities and goal alignment and has a mean of 4.91 (SD = 1.37). This would indicate that senior management believe that they play a key role in aligning sales and marketing activities and are able to influence the relationship. Marketing intelligence process has a mean of 4.60 (SD = 1.11). This measure considers the inclusion of sales in the collection of market intelligence and the dissemination of market intelligence around the organisation. The findings indicate that a number of senior managers in the sample believe that they have an inclusive market intelligence system.

The sampled organisations responded positively to the questions on market orientation ($M = 5.14$, SD = .74) indicating that the majority believed that they were market orientated. Collaboration between sales and marketing considers cross-functional teamwork and goal alignment and has a mean of 5.31 (SD = 1.21). It would appear that goal alignment and cross-functional working are key elements in building collaboration between sales and marketing, and the majority of the sampled organisations believe that they were operating in a collaborative manner because they observed these two activities. The measure of business performance had a mean of 4.66 (SD = 1.08) indicating that the majority of the businesses sampled believed that they were performing above average for their industry.

Model testing

In Table 4 we report the regression analyses findings of the key relationships that are shown in Figure 1. H1 proposes a positive relationship between market orientation and business performance and the results indicate that this relationship is significant and therefore the hypothesis is accepted. H2 examines the relationship between collaboration between sales and marketing and business performance, and finds there is a positive and significant relationship between the two. These results would indicate that both these variables have a significant impact on business performance.

Hypotheses H3, H4, and H8 consider the relationships between collaboration between sales and marketing, management attitudes towards coordination, and market intelligence system and market orientation. All these relationships have been shown to have significant impact on market orientation and the hypotheses have been accepted. Hypotheses H5 and H7 investigate the relationship between collaboration between sales and marketing, and

Table 4. Direct effect on dependent variables.

Dependent Direct effect on dependent variables	Independent	B	Beta	R	Adjusted R2	F	Sig. of F	t	p
Business performance	Market orientation H1	.525	.359	.544	.289	30.072	.000	4.159	.000
	Collaboration between sales and marketing H2	.230	.126						2.908	.004
Market orientation	Collaboration between sales and marketing H3	.096	.177	.698	.476	44.894	.000	2.282	.024
	Management attitudes towards coordination H4	.151	.241					2.921	.004
	Market intelligence H8	.257	.403					5.315	.000
Collaboration between sales and marketing	Management attitudes towards coordination H5	.361	.416	.684	.460	62.813	.000	5.916	.000
	Market intelligence H7	.378	.373					5.301	.000
Market intelligence	Management attitudes towards coordination H6	.426	.499	.499	.244	47.674	.000	6.905	.000

management attitudes towards coordination and market intelligence system. The results indicate that these two variables have a positive and significant relationship with collaboration between sales and marketing and therefore these hypotheses have been accepted. H6 examines the relationship between management attitudes towards coordination and marketing intelligence process and finds a positive and significant relationship. Therefore the hypothesis is accepted, indicating that management attitudes to coordination will have an impact on the collection, storage, and dissemination of market intelligence across the organisation.

Discussion and implications

The primary aim of this paper was to discover whether improvements in collaboration between sales and marketing have an impact on market orientation and/or business performance, as well as to discover the roles that an effective market intelligence system and management attitudes towards coordination have on the other elements in the interface. The research expected to find a positive relationship between market intelligence system and market orientation as this has been established in previous research (e.g. Tadepalli & Avila, 1999). Further, it was expected that there would be a positive relationship between management attitudes towards coordination and market orientation (e.g. Slater & Narver, 1994). These expected relationships were confirmed by the findings from this research. We also discovered that these two variables had a positive and significant effect on collaboration between sales and marketing. This is an important finding because the same variables that impact on market orientation also influence collaboration between sales and marketing and may therefore be used to improve this relationship.

The internal relationship between sales and marketing is not always a supportive one. There have been examples of sales and marketing competing with each other for resources and working against each other (Kotler et al., 2006), for example, sales ignoring marketing leads and marketing launching new products before sales have cleared the old lines. Further, internal groups who are in competition with each other have been found to withhold information (Jaworski & Kohli, 1993), obstruct decision making (Ruekert & Walker, 1987), and undertake poor quality planning (Menon et al., 1996). These elements are not conducive to a market orientation. Other writers have suggested that the primary difficulty in creating collaboration between sales and marketing has been the setting of separate goals and objectives; sales with a short-term perspective and marketing with a longer-term one (e.g. Olson, Cravens, & Slater, 2001; Strahle, Spiro, & Acito, 1996). The result is that these two functions have now been described as exhibiting significant levels of distrust and conflict (e.g. Dewsnap & Jobber, 2000; Kotler et al., 2006; Rouzies et al., 2005) that work against a clear customer focus and a market orientation.

Some writers have suggested that the sales and marketing interface may be improved through co-location of sales and marketing activities (Dewsnap & Jobber, 2000; Rouzies et al., 2005), or through job rotation (Kotler et al., 2006) or the creation of cross-functional teams (Rouzies et al., 2005). However, these approaches may be an over-reaction to a complex problem and a change in the organisation's thought processes may be more effective. If management attitudes towards coordination can be positive and effort is expended in trying to align sales and marketing goals, creating an *esprit de corps* and achieving a mutual understanding, then not only will sales and marketing collaboration be enhanced, but market orientation and marketing intelligence processes will also be improved. Senior managers have a critical role to play in creating the culture of the organisation, the direction that the organisation would like to take, and encouraging a market orientated approach.

This research has also found that an effective marketing intelligence process can have a considerable impact in improving the relationship between sales and marketing as well as driving a market orientation. Effective market intelligence gathering plays an increasingly important role in informing strategic decision making within a market orientated organisation (Piercy & Lane, 2005). Market intelligence is created through gathering data from a range of sources including the marketplace and research has shown that sales are a relevant and valid source of up-to-date information about customers and competitors (Festervand, Grove, & Reidenbach, 1988). Combining information from sales and marketing sources and disseminating it back to both functions promotes collaboration and sharing. Market intelligence collection from the sales force may contribute little additional cost to the market budget. However, in many organisations, there does not appear to be a recognised process for integrating this type of information into market intelligence systems (Capron & Hulland, 1999). Further, to be successfully market orientated an organisation should be customer focused. As salespeople are in a strong position to provide early insights into the activities of competitors, as well as other changes in the marketplace they are ideally suited to assist the organisation to be market responsive. An effective market intelligence system is an important element in creating market orientation and providing an activity upon which sales and marketing can collaborate.

Improvements in collaboration between sales and marketing have a significant impact on market orientation. This result may be expected as part of effective market orientation is the development of inter-function cooperation (e.g. Narver & Slater, 1990), but sales and marketing collaboration may have been overlooked as it is a 'within-function' relationship. To establish a strong market orientation organisations require managers to have a positive attitude towards coordination, and an effective market intelligence system and collaboration between sales and marketing. Further, the research confirmed that not only does market orientation have a beneficial impact on business performance (e.g. Slater & Narver, 2000), but it was also established that improvements in the relationship between sales and marketing have a direct and positive impact on business performance, as well as strengthening market orientation.

In a context of increasing competition between organisations in the business-to-business environment organisations are focusing on improving their customer focus to improve their performance. This research examines the interrelationship between four internal factors – management attitudes towards coordination, market intelligence systems, collaboration between sales and marketing, and market orientation – and finds that not only should organisations work to improve inter-functional cooperation across the organisation in general to create market orientation, but they should specifically focus on the sometimes problematical relationship between sales and marketing. If senior managers can adopt a positive approach towards coordination between functions and encourage sales and marketing to focus on the customer, their competitors, and build on coordinated activities they should experience improvements not only in their market orientation, but also directly in their business performance. The research also provides confirmation that the variable of market intelligence system may be used to leverage improvements in both collaboration between sales and marketing and contribute to a market orientation.

Further research and limitations

This research provides an initial basis for future research into the importance of collaboration between sales and marketing in B2B organisations in improving market orientation, but there are several possible limitations to the research. The measure for business performance was self-reported and therefore may be liable to over-inflation by the respondents. However, this type of measure has been used successfully in other studies. In addition, the questionnaires were completed by the Senior Executive/Managing Director of the organisation and not by the Sales and Marketing Managers and therefore may contain a biased view of the complex relationship between sales and marketing. Finally, there is a possibility of common method bias as there was a single respondent from each organisation. This research should now be extended to consider the impact of sales and marketing collaboration on market orientation in small and medium sized enterprises, as well as on organisations operating outside the UK.

References

Armstrong, J.S., & Overton, T.S. (1977). Estimating nonresponse bias in mail surveys. *Journal of Marketing Research, 14*(August), 396–402.

Behrman, D.N., & Perreault, W.D., Jr. (1982). Measuring the performance of industrial salespersons. *Journal of Business Research, 10*(3), 335–370.

Bryman, A. (2001). *Social research methods.* Oxford: Oxford University Press.

Capron, L., & Hulland, H. (1999). Redeployment of brands, sales forces, and general marketing management expertise following horizontal acquisitions: A resource-based view. *Journal of Marketing, 63*(April), 41–54.

Churchill, G.A., Jr, & Iacobucci, D. (2002). *Marketing research methodological foundations* (8th ed.). Mason: South-Western.

Corstjens, J., & Corstjens, M. (1999). *Store wars.* Chichester: John Wiley & Sons.

Cross, J., Hartley, S.W., Rudelius, W., & Vassey, M.J. (2001). Sales force activities and marketing strategies in industrial firms: Relationships and implications. *Journal of Personal Selling and Sales Management, 21*(3), 199–206.

Dewsnap, B., & Jobber, D. (2000). The sales–marketing interface in consumer packaged-goods companies: A conceptual framework. *Journal of Personal Selling and Sales Management, 20*(2), 109–119.

Donath, B. (2004). 10 tips help align sales and marketing teams. *Marketing News, 38*(12), 5–7.

Doyle, P. (2002). *Marketing management and strategy* (3rd ed.). Harlow: Financial Times Prentice Hall.

Evans, K.R., & Schlacter, J.L. (1985). The role of sales managers and salespeople in a marketing information system. *Journal of Personal Selling and Sales Management, 5*(November), 49–55.

Festervand, T.A., Grove, S.J., & Reidenbach, R.E. (1988). The sales force as a marketing intelligence system. *Journal of Business and Industrial Marketing, 3*(1), 53–59.

Grove, S.J., Carlson, L., & Dorsch, M.J. (1992). Addressing services' intangibility through integrated marketing communication: An exploratory study. *Journal of Service Marketing, 16*(5), 393–411.

Harris, L.C., & Ogbonna, E. (2000). The responses of front-line employees to market-oriented culture change. *European Journal of Marketing, 34*(3/4), 318–340.

Homburg, C., & Jensen, O. (2007). The thought worlds of marketing and sales: Which differences make a difference? *Journal of Marketing, 71*(3), 124–142.

Homburg, C., Workman, J.P., Jr, & Jensen, O. (2000). Fundamental changes in marketing organization: The movement toward a customer-focused organizational structure. *Journal of the Academy of Marketing Science, 28*(4), 459–478.

Houston, M.J., & Nevin, F.R. (1977). The effects of source and appeal on mail survey response patterns. *Journal of Marketing Research, 14*(30), 374–378.

Hult, G.T.M., Ketchen, D.J., Jr, & Slater, S.F. (2002). A longitudinal study of the learning climate and cycle time in supply chains. *Journal of Business and Industrial Marketing, 17*(4), 302–323.

Jaworski, B.J., & Kohli, A.K. (1993). Market orientation: Antecedents and consequences. *Journal of Marketing, 57*(July), 53–70.

Khan, K.B. (1996). Interdepartmental Integration: A definition with implications for product development performance. *Journal of Product Innovation Management, 13*(2), 137–151.

Kohli, A.K., & Jaworski, B.J. (1990). Market orientation: The construct, research propositions, and managerial implications. *Journal of Marketing, 54*(April), 1–18.

Kotler, P., Rackham, N., & Krishnaswamy, S. (2006). Ending the war between sales & marketing. *Harvard Business Review, 84*(7/8), 68–78.

Le Meunier-FitzHugh, K., & Piercy, N.F. (2006). Integrating marketing intelligence sources: Reconsidering the role of the salesforce. *International Journal of Market Research, 48*(6), 699–719.

Maltz, E., & Kohli, A.K. (2000). Reducing marketing's conflict with other functions: The differential effects of integrating mechanisms. *Journal of the Academy of Marketing Science, 28*(4), 479–492.

Menon, A., Bharadwaj, S.G., & Howell, R. (1996). The quality and effectiveness of marketing strategy: Effects of functional and dysfunctional conflict in intraorganizational relationship. *Journal of the Academy of Marketing Science, 24*(4), 299–313.

Morgan, R.E., & Turnell, C.R. (2003). Market-based organisational learning and market performance gains. *British Journal of Management, 14*(3), 255–274.

Moser, C.A., & Kalton, G. (1971). *Survey methods in social investigation* (2nd ed.). London: Heinemann.

Narver, J.C., & Slater, S.F. (1990). The effect of a market orientation on business profitability. *Journal of Marketing, 54*(October), 20–35.

Olson, E.M., Cravens, D.W., & Slater, S.F. (2001). Competitiveness and sales management: A marriage of strategies. *Business Horizons, 44*(March–April), 25–30.

Piercy, N.F., & Lane, N. (2005). Strategic imperatives of transformation in the conventional sales organization. *Journal of Change Management, 5*(3), 249–266.

Pulendran, S., Speed, R., & Widing, R.E., III. (2003). Marketing planning, market orientation and business performance. *European Journal of Marketing, 37*(3/4), 476–497.

Reid, M., Luxton, S., & Mavondo, F. (2005). The relationship between integrated marketing communications, market orientation and brand orientation. *Journal of Advertising, 34*(4), 11–23.

Robinson, J.P., Shaver, P.R., & Wrightsman, L.S. (1991). Criteria for scale selection and evaluation. In J.P. Robinson, P.R. Shaver, & S. le Wrightsman (Eds.), *Measures of personality and social psychological attitudes* (pp. 1–16). San Diego, CA: Academic Press.

Rouzies, D., Anderson, E., Kohli, A.K., Michaels, R.E., Weitz, B.A., & Zoltners, A.A. (2005). Sales and marketing integration: A proposed framework. *Journal of Personal Selling and Sales Management, 15*(2), 113–122.

Ruekert, R.W., & Walker, O.C., Jr. (1987). Marketing's interaction with other functional units: A conceptual frame work and empirical evidence. *Journal of Marketing, 51*(1), 1–19.

Schmonsees, R.J. (2006). *Escaping the black hole: Minimizing the damage from marketing–sales disconnect.* Mason: Thomson South-Western.

Shapiro, B. (1988). What the hell is market oriented? *Harvard Business Review, 66*(6), 119–125.

Siguaw, J.A., Brown, G., & Widing, R.E., II. (1994). The influence of the market orientation of the firm on sales force behaviour and attitudes. *Journal of Market Research, 16*(February), 106–116.

Simkin, L. (2002). Tackling implementation impediments to marketing planning. *Marketing Intelligence and Planning, 20*(2), 120–126.

Sinkula, J.M., Baker, W.E., & Noordewier, T. (1997). A framework for market-based organisational learning: Linking value, knowledge, and behaviour. *Journal of the Academy of Marketing Science, 25*(4), 305–318.

Slater, S.F., & Narver, J.C. (1994). Market orientation, customer value, and superior performance. *Business Horizons, 37*(March–April), 22–28.

Slater, S.F., & Narver, J.C. (2000). The positive effect of a market orientation on business profitability: A balanced replication. *Journal of Business Research, 48*(1), 69–73.

Slotegraaf, R.J., & Dickson, P.R. (2004). The paradox of a marketing planning capability. *Journal of the Academy of Marketing Science, 32*(4), 371–385.

Small and medium enterprise definitions. Retrieved July 30, 2004 from http://www.sbs.gov.uk/analytical/statistics/smedefs.php

Strahle, W.M., Spiro, R.L., & Acito, F. (1996). Marketing and sales: Strategic alignment and functional implementation. *Journal of Personal Selling and Sales Management, 16*(1), 1–20.

Tadepalli, R., & Avila, R.A. (1999). Market orientation and the marketing strategy process. *Journal of Marketing Theory and Practice*, 7(2), 69–82.

Webster, F.E., Jr. (1988). The rediscovery of the marketing concept. *Business Horizons*, 52(May–June), 29–39.

Webster, F.E., Jr. (1997). The future role of marketing in the organization. In D.R. Lehman & K.E. Jocz (Eds.), *Reflections on the future of marketing: Practice and education* (pp. 39–66). Cambridge: Marketing Science Institute.

Appendix 1. Scales items for construct measure

Construct	Items	Adapted from
Business performance 1 = Needs improvement 7 = Outstanding	How successful is the organisation at generating a high level of sales revenue? How successful is the organisation at generating high market share? How successful is the organisation at selling those products with the highest profit margins? How successful is the organisation at exceeding all sales targets and objectives during the year? How successful is the organisation at generating sales of new products? How successful is the organisation at producing sales with long-term profitability?	Behrman and Perreault (1982)
Market orientation 1 = Not at all 7 = To an extreme extent Customer orientation	Sales and marketing objectives are driven primarily by customer satisfaction. We constantly review our level of commitment toserving our customer needs Our strategy for competitive advantage is based on our understanding of our customer's needs. Our marketing strategies are driven by our belief that we can create greater value for customers. We measure customer satisfaction systematically and frequently. We give close attention to after sales service. Senior management regularly visits our current and prospective customers.	Narver and Slater (1990)
Inter-functional coordination	Sales and marketing are integrated when servicing our target market(s). We share resources between sales and marketing. We freely communicate information about successful and unsuccessful customer experiences between sales and marketing. Sales and marketing staff understand how they can contribute to creating customer value.	

Appendix 1. – *continued*

Construct	Items	Adapted from
Competitive orientation	Within our business, our sales people regularly share information concerning competitors' strategy. We rapidly respond to competitors actions that threaten us. Senior management regularly discusses competitors' strengths and strategies.	
Collaboration between sales and marketing 1 = Strongly disagree 7 = Strongly agree	A team sprit pervades sales and marketing. Sales and marketing share the same goals.	Hult et al. (2002)
Market intelligence system 1 = Very infrequently 7 = Very frequently	How frequently does the organisation use sales as a source of information? How frequently does the organisation feedback on the use of the market information from sales? How frequently does the organisation use marketing information as part of sales performance evaluation?	Evans and Schlacter (1985)
1 = Strongly disagree 7 = Strongly agree	Marketing personnel spend time discussing customers' future needs with the sales department. There is a lot of communications between marketing and the sales department concerning market development. When the sales department finds out something important about customers, it is quick to alert other departments.	Sinkula, Baker, and Noordewier (1997)
Management attitudes towards coordination 1 = Not at all 7 = To a great extent	Senior management ensures that the sales and marketing goals are closely aligned. To what degree does senior management ensure that the activities of the sales and marketing departments are well coordinated?	New Scale

Strategizing the sales organization

Nikala Lane and Nigel Piercy

This paper sets out to provide a managerial framework into which new research
findings and company characteristics can be fitted for executives implementing the
changes that will develop a strategic sales organization. We propose a framework to
identify the important though inter-related issues to be considered by executives in
managing the sales organization transformation process. This framework examines two
sets of issues: immediate managerial concerns in the strategizing process, and broader
organizational consequences. Managerial concerns close to the strategizing process
include: involvement in business and marketing strategy decisions; intelligence as a
basis for added value; integration of cross-functional contributions to customer value;
internal marketing of customer priorities to internal departments and employees; and
building the new types of sales organization infrastructure that will support a new
strategic role. Broader organizational consequences to consider include: inspiration or
leadership at several levels; influence over important issues of strategic direction;
integrity in ethical standards and corporate social responsibility initiatives; and, an
international perspective on managing sales and customers.

The objective of this article is to propose a managerial framework for use by executives in
appraising the evolution in the role of the sales organization in their companies, and as a
checklist for considering the range of factors which may be relevant. While the idea of the
strategic sales organization and a shift in sales functions from transaction to relationship
and value has been discussed for some time, our contribution is to attempt an integrative
model for practical application.

The structure of the paper involves first, summarizing the rationale that underpins the
transformation of the traditional sales organization to align it better with the needs of
business and marketing strategy, leading to a description of the integrative model we have
developed for executive use. The remainder of the article teases out a little more detail
about the themes we propose need to be addressed in sales organization transformation, as
identified in the integrative model.

We do not suggest that the model is a complete representation of the sales organization
transformation process, rather that it provides a loose framework of important related
issues, into which new research findings may be fitted and the individual characteristics of
different companies accommodated to provide executives with a useful operational tool.

A rationale for sales organization transformation

A starting point in examining the drivers and priorities on sales organization change for a specific company may be facilitated by reviewing the types of pressure illustrated in Figure 1. This provides a framework for establishing priorities.

New marketing strategies and business models

For some time sales organizations in companies have been under powerful company and customer forces that have re-shaped the sales force role and operation (e.g. see Jones, Brown, Zoltners, & Weitz, 2005). Major forces acting to re-shape the sales function in organizations are summarized in Figure 1. In particular, the implementation of new types of marketing strategy and business model, driven by customer relationships and value, requires the realignment of sales processes with the strategy – many sales organizations have inherited structures and processes that were set up to do a quite different, largely transactional, job.

Competition from multiple/direct channels

At the same time, multi-channelling and the growth in Internet-based direct channels are substituting for many traditional sales activities, so direct channels compete with the traditional salesperson.

For instance, Dell Computers is an Internet-based company – the majority of sales and service provisions are on the Web. Nonetheless, Dell maintains both account executives in the field as well as internal salespeople in branches, because their view is that the technology exists to free salespeople to sell and develop customer relationships, not to process orders (which the technology generally does better and cheaper). Indeed, part of Dell's fight-back against the decline of its direct model in delivering sales growth is developing multiple, global sales channels.

Figure 1.   Pressures on the sales organization.

Stringent productivity and efficiency initiatives

Moreover, in many situations management wants more for less – the days of throwing money at marketplace problems have gone for most companies, and the issue is enhanced productivity. Higher productivity in sales is very attractive to management if it achieves both top line and bottom line effects at the same time – sell more, cheaper, and profit rises as well as volume. In fact, evidence from the USA suggests that many senior managers are dissatisfied with the productivity of their sales organizations, and many see sales force cost poorly aligned with their strategic goals (Deloitte Touche Development, 2005).

Escalating and more complex customer demands

One of the most dramatic changes in business-to-business marketing in the twenty-first century has been the breath-taking escalation in the demands for enhanced service, new types of relationships, and greater added value by business-to-business customers of all kinds. The HR Chally consultancy's *Chally world class sales excellence research report* (HR Chally, 2006) investigates the views of corporate purchasers and their expectations for the relationship with the salesperson from a supplier, and mandates that the seller will: (1) *be personally accountable for our desired results* – the sales contact with the supplier is expected to be committed to the customer and accountable for achievement; (2) *understand our business* – to be able to add value, the supplier must understand the customer's competencies, strategies, challenges, and organizational culture; (3) *be on our side* – the salesperson must be the customer's advocate in his/her own organization, and operate through the policies and politics to focus on the customer's needs; (4) *design the right applications* – the salesperson is expected to think beyond technical features and functions to the implementation of the product or service in the customer's environment, thinking beyond the transaction to the customer's end state; (5) *be easily accessible* – customers expect salespeople to be constantly connected and within reach; (6) *solve our problems* – customers no longer buy products or services, they buy solutions to their business problems, and expect salespeople to diagnose, prescribe, and resolve their issues, not just sell them products; and, (7) *be creative in responding to our needs* – buyers expect salespeople to be innovators, who bring them new ideas to solve problems, so creativity is a major source of added value.

HR Chally argues persuasively that these qualities characterize how world class sales forces are distinguished in the eyes of their customers. They describe a customer environment which is radically different from the transactional selling approaches of the past, and which poses substantially different management challenges in managing business-to-business customer relationships. The sales and service organizations which meet these customer demands and expectations and develop sustainable and attractive customer relationships are likely to look very different to those of the past, and to work very differently.

Indeed, in many sectors, traditional sales models may be actually obsolete as a result of growing customer sophistication. For example, in the pharmaceuticals business, high sales pressure placed on doctors to prescribe new drugs has resulted in formal training courses in medical schools to teach future doctors how to resist sales pitches (Weintraub, 2008). This is symptomatic of the search by the pharmaceutical industry for new and better ways to get to market. Companies like Pfizer, Wyeth, Novartis, and GlaxoSmithKlein recognize that the era of 'hard sell' is over in this sector and are working to develop new sales models.

Writing in *Harvard Business Review*, Thomas Stewart (2006, p. 10) summarizes the new and emerging role for the sales organization in these situations in the following terms:

> Selling is changing fast and in such a way that sales teams have become strategic resources. When corporations strive to become customer focused, salespeople move to the foreground; engineers recede. As companies go to market with increasingly complex bundles of products and services, their representatives cease to be mere order takers (most orders are placed online, anyway) and become relationship managers.

Our logic is that such fundamental changes in the requirements of business customers mandate a strategic response from sellers that is more robust than simple acquiescence to demands for lower prices and higher service levels. The challenge is to reposition sales as a core part of a company's competitiveness, where the sales organization is closely integrated into a company's business strategy (Stephens, 2003).

In summary, the pattern of changes encouraging many organizations to reconsider the configuration of their sales and customer-facing resources can be summarized in the following terms:

> Today's competitive environment demands a radically different approach. Specifically, the ability of firms to exploit the true potential of the sales organization requires that company executives adopt a new mindset about the role of the selling function within the firm, how the sales force is managed, and what salespeople are expected to produce. The sales function must serve as a dynamic source of value creation and innovation within the firm. (The Sales Educators, 2006, p. 1)

Fulfilling that potential and delivering value creation and innovation to a company is likely to require more than the conventional and traditional sales department.

An integrative model of sales organization transformation

In truth, we still have a lot to learn about the shape and operation of the genuinely strategic sales organization. As a basis for management analysis and planning, Figure 2 provides a view of what we believe to be among the most important imperatives and mandates for developing and evaluating a strategic sales organization.

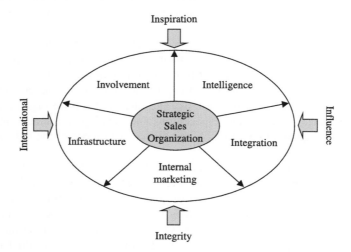

Figure 2. A framework for managing the strategic sales organization transformation. Source: Adapted from Piercy and Lane (2009).

The framework we propose in Figure 2 suggests two groups of factors to be considered. The first group is related to the operational content of a strategic sales role, while the second group addresses broader organizational mandates.

Our first group of managerial concerns in evaluating the strategic role of the sales organization include: *involvement* – placing the sales organization in the centre of the business and marketing strategy debate in companies and aligning sales operations with strategic direction; *intelligence* – building customer knowledge as a strategic resource critical both to strategy formulation and to building added-value strategies with major customers though superior market sensing; *integration* – establishing the cross-functional relationships necessary to lead processes which define, develop, and deliver superior value propositions to customers, and managing the interfaces between functions and business units impacting on service and value as it is perceived by customers; *internal marketing* – using sales resources to 'sell' the customer across functional and divisional boundaries within the company and across organizational boundaries with partner companies, to achieve seamless value delivery for customers; and, *infrastructure* – developing the structure and processes needed to manage sales and account management organizations to match customer relationship requirements and to build competitive advantage – compensation systems, evaluation systems, and training and development investments have to be designed to align with relationship and partnership, not the transactional focus of the past.

These challenges are the most immediate in assessing how to build the sales organization as an effective strategic force in a company. However, there are also other broader drivers of organizational change which demand attention. These broader mandates include: *inspiration* – part of the outcome of strategizing the sales organization should be to renew the ability of those who manage key external relationships with customers to inspire and provide leadership within the business; *influence* – a test of whether sales as a strategic function is being taken seriously in exerting influence over the company's strategic agenda and the key decisions which are made; *integrity* – there has never been a time when scrutiny of the ethical and responsible behaviour of companies was greater, and when the cost of being judged unethical or irresponsible was higher, and this may be the highest priority in new types of buyer–seller relationship (Galea, 2006); and, *international* – the globalization of markets, the emergence of global customers, and the spread of international competition mandates an international perspective on how we manage customer relationships in domestic and overseas markets.

These themes are examined as the themes in managing sales organization transformation. We do not imply that all are likely to be of equal importance in a specific situation, but that the model overall provides a view of the potentially important issues for managers to consider.

Themes in managing sales organization transformation

Involvement

The first theme identified in our strategic sales model (Figure 2) is involvement, in the sense of sales involvement in the generation and evaluation of marketing and business strategy, rather than just being a tactical operation responsible for implementing or executing strategies created by others. In other words, the imperative is putting sales back into the business strategy process.

There are several compelling reasons why putting the sales voice back in the strategy debate may be advantageous. First, many of the most significant resource investment decisions actually hinge on the assumptions we make about the company's customer base – its customer portfolio. Second, the shape of the customer portfolio has a direct impact on the profit opportunities which are open to a company. Third, many of the most serious business risks companies face relate to the dependence they have on certain parts of the customer portfolio. Fourth, modern markets are increasingly characterized by fragmentation and granularity, so just looking at averages like market share and overall growth rates blinds executives to the most important emerging trends, opportunities, and threats.

In fact, involvement of the sales organization in strategy has two aspects. The *first* strategic sales issue is concerned with developing a perspective on sales relationships which does not focus simply on the tactical management of transactional selling processes, but examines the different relationships that may be formed with different types of customers as the basis for long-term business development (Olson, Cravens, & Slater, 2001). This implies a new appraisal of the activities and processes required to enhance and sustain value delivery to customers through the sales organization.

The *second* strategic sales issue is concerned with the role of sales and account management in interpreting the customer environment as a basis for strategic decisions. As the costs of dealing with major customers continue to increase, companies face major choices in where they choose to invest resources in developing a customer relationship, and where they choose not to invest. With large customers in particular, the risks in investment or disinvestment are high, and it is likely that the intelligence-gathering and market-sensing capabilities of the sales and account organization will play a growing role in influencing strategic decisions about resource allocation in the customer portfolio.

We propose a simple model of the customer portfolio in Figure 3, to provide an accessible approach to classifying different customer types (direct channel customers, middle market customers, major accounts, and strategic accounts) on the basis of their sales

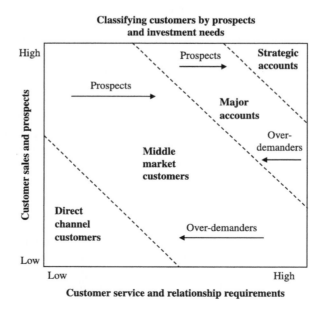

Figure 3. Modelling the customer portfolio as an investment matrix. Source: Adapted from Piercy and Lane (2009).

and prospects and service and relationship investment requirements. However, in addition to evaluating the likely sales results of alternative investments, the customer portfolio is also linked to more fundamental issues of the quality of sales in terms of dependence and risk with major and strategic accounts. We suggest in Figure 4 that the balance of dependence between buyer and seller and the quality of the buyer–seller relationship impact on sales expectations and indicate the level of business risk being assumed and hence the implications for longer-term seller profitability. There are certainly research indications that dominant customers can use their power over highly dependent partners to improve their own performance at the expense of weaker members of the value chain – in such cases while customers are making performance gains through closer supplier relationships, suppliers do not necessarily reap reciprocal benefits (Fink, Feldman, & Hatten, 2007).

For example, the risks of assuming customer loyalty may be considerable. One of the first pieces of news received by the incoming CEO of British steel company Corus in 2009 was from four major steel producers who were responsible for buying nearly 80% of the steel from his Redcar plant in Teeside. The consortium of Italian, Korean, Swiss, and Argentinean customers had decided unilaterally to dishonour their 10 year contract with Corus (which had five years left to run), because they could get cheaper steel elsewhere. The deal with Corus was only attractive to these customers when steel prices were high. Corus is unlikely to be able to find new customers for this volume of steel, and is likely to have to close the plant as a result (Tighe, 2009).

Certainly a customer portfolio analysis is increasingly placing sales and marketing executives in the position of identifying business opportunities to decline and avoid as well as those to pursue, and when to exit from a customer relationship as well as when to enter one. For example, as part of its attempts to rebuild profitability in its Global Services business, British Telecom is looking deliberately to reduce revenue by 4–5% because it is becoming more selective about the customer contracts it will enter. Two of the existing major Global Services customers forced BT to take a £1.3 billion charge against fourth quarter earnings. The company is looking to rethink the optimistic assumptions it makes about the attractiveness of global customers and to focus more on profitability and less on volume (Parker, Cohen, & Burgess, 2009).

Involvement in business and marketing strategy decisions is likely to involve the sales organization in a different domain with different priorities to those of the transactional, implementation-focus of the past, and provides a first test of the strategizing of the sales role.

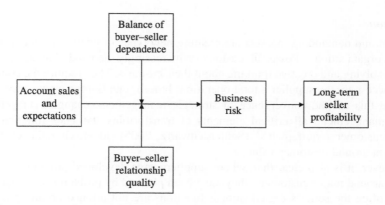

Figure 4.   Customer dependence and business risk.

Intelligence

A second theme in developing the strategic sales organization is intelligence – knowledge and understanding of the market that underpins the ability to identify value-creating opportunities for the business.

This is based on two pieces of logic. First, we live in a world where intense market knowledge and superior understanding underpins competitive advantage. At its simplest, wherever you go, it appears when you look at the winners that 'those who know more, make more'. Second, too much information inside companies is about themselves (e.g. market research studies of brands and market share) and is essentially out-of-date by the time anyone gets it because it is historical (e.g. customer relationship management system data on past sales to existing customers is not a great basis for insight into the future). By virtue of its deep links into the marketplace, the strategic sales organization can impact on business performance by enhancing management understanding of how markets operate and how they are changing based on real intelligence. The challenge is bringing customer issues into the boardroom in a way which marketing departments have largely failed to do – a survey of large US companies shows that their boards spend less than 10% of their time discussing customer-related issues (McGovern, Court, Quelch, & Crawford, 2004).

A first concern is what it takes to develop a higher 'market IQ' through superior market sensing capabilities, and specific points where the intelligence capabilities of the strategic sales organization impact: underlining changing market definitions and the implications, highlighting changing market structures and sales channels and what they mean for business strategy, building market pictures to show how market change creates strategic opportunities, and providing customer insight when managers talk about their strengths and weaknesses and the opportunities and threats in the market. These approaches provide the structure to go from simply having information, to identifying implications and opportunities to be addressed.

However, then we can turn to the second and equally significant aspect of intelligence for the strategic sales organization – the impact of market intelligence on building added value in dealing with major customers. For example, Figure 5 suggests the changing emphasis on sales relationships from transactional and relational investments to a strategic focus on making the customer more profitable in the customer's end-use markets. There is abundant evidence that the priority for major customers is performance enhancement rather than simply buying products.

Integration

Turbulent and demanding markets are creating new types of challenges for managers in supplier organizations. Powerful customers increasingly demand that sellers provide problem-solving and creative thinking about their business. They require the commitment of, and access to, the supplier's total operation. Indeed, one European executive recently described this as 'the convergence of strategic management, change management and process management, all critical elements of transforming the sales function to meet today's customer requirements' (Seidenschwartz, 2005), identifying the challenge of integration around customer value.

However, it is also clear that, where suppliers have developed programmes of value creation around major customers, they have been plagued by problems of 'organizational drag' – often the seller's organizational functions are not aligned around processes of creating and delivering customer value (Koerner, 2005). Major retailers across the world

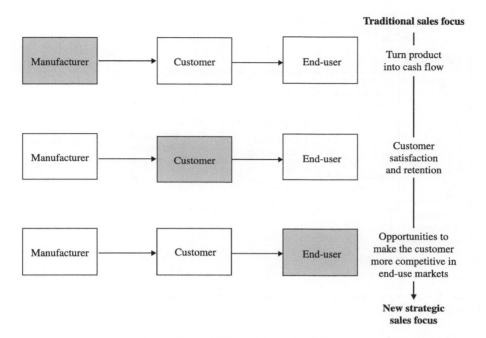

Figure 5. Changing the emphasis in strategic sales from product to value. Source: Adapted from Piercy and Lane (2009).

emphasize supplier organizational structure and culture as key obstacles to improving customer management effectiveness (IBM, 2005).

Yet traditional 'command and control' company organizations continue to create rigid, hierarchical organizations which do not permit the merging of systems, activities, and people. Success in the new marketplace increasingly demands the careful and systematic integration of a company's entire set of capabilities into a seamless system that delivers superior customer value – what we have called elsewhere 'total integrated marketing' (Hulbert, Capon, & Piercy, 2002). Our logic is based on the observation that superior performing companies seem to share one simple yet vital characteristic: they get their act together around the things that matter most to their customers, and they make a totally integrated offer of superior value in customer terms.

It is likely that one of the most critical roles of the strategic sales organization will be in managing processes of customer value definition, development, and delivery that cut across functional interfaces and organizational boundaries to build real customer focus. Many of the barriers to developing and delivering superior customer value come from the characteristics of supplier organizations. The new challenge mandates effective approaches to cross-functional integration around value processes. Rather than managing only the interface with the customer, the strategic sales force must cope with a range of interfaces with internal functions and departments, and increasingly partner organizations, to deliver value seamlessly to customers.

For example, when Sam Palmisano took over as CEO at IBM, he conducted a painful overhaul of the 38,000 person sales force (Hamm, 2005, 2008). In the 1990s salespeople representing the various IBM business units were essentially on their own – looking for good opportunities to sell individual products or services. Palmisano has 'reintegrated'

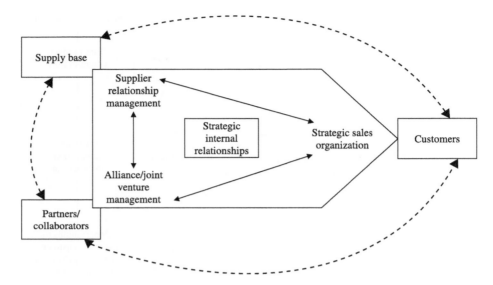

Figure 6. Strategic internal and external relationships. Source: Adapted from Piercy and Lane (2009).

IBM in front of customers by bringing together specialists from computers, software, consulting, and even research into teams that meet with customers to help solve their business problems and develop new business strategies. People who do not work well with others get replaced. Collaborating with customers, suppliers, and even rivals is part of his plan to invent new technologies to create new markets, placing a far greater emphasis on strategic sales relationships compared to traditional sales and marketing activities.

Importantly, while traditionally sales has managed external relationships – primarily with customers – it is likely that success in the future will depend on new types of skill and capabilities in managing strategic internal relationships. For example, Figure 6 illustrates the need for integration between three sets of decision makers to deliver superior customer value: the strategic sales organization in its relationship with customers; supplier relationship management in its relationships with the supply base; and, alliance/joint venture management in relationships with external partners and collaborators. Factoring in the additional complexity that suppliers, collaborators, and customers in a business-to-business market face underlines the complexity faced in integration around customer value strategies.

Internal marketing

A strategic approach to the role of sales in managing customer value underlines the importance of positioning and 'selling' the customer value strategy inside the organization. The internal marketplace is company employees and managers (and increasingly partner organizations' employees and managers) whose attitudes, beliefs, and behaviour impact on customers and influence our ability to keep service and relationship promises. For example, we often find that there are differences between internal market and external market criteria of what 'matters' – the priorities of people in the 'back office' or the factory may conflict with those of the external customer.

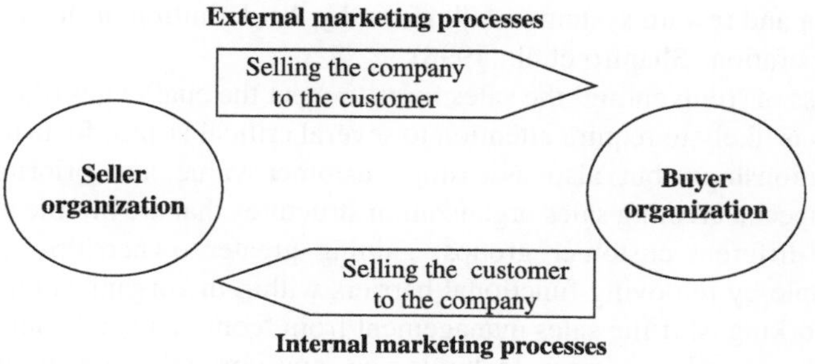

Figure 7.   Internal and external marketing roles. Source: Adapted from Piercy and Lane (2009).

One role of the strategic sales organization is likely to be 'selling' the customer to employees and managers, as a basis for understanding customer priorities and the importance of meeting them, as an activity that parallels conventional sales and marketing efforts, as suggested in Figure 7. Sales organizations are familiar with the idea that what they are actually selling to customers is the company – its reputation, standing, capabilities, and so on – more than just products. The internal marketing parallel is selling the customer to the company – to the internal market of employees, managers, and partner organizations.

Clearly, much depends on exactly how you define what is internal marketing, but research at Northwestern University in the USA has found internal marketing to be one of the top three determinants of a company's financial performance – quite simply, companies with better integration of internal and external market processes report better financial results (Chang, 2005). Other studies suggest that a lot of organizations are struggling to deliver their value propositions to external customers because of inadequate investment in the internal marketplace and a lack of internal marketing (*Marketing Week*, 2003).

Infrastructure

The role of the transforming sales organization is unlikely to be implemented effectively through traditional salesforce structures and processes – they were not set up to do this job. In fact, Shapiro, Slywotsky, and Doyle (1998, p. 3) suggested, some time ago, that 'most established sales forces are in deep trouble. They were designed for a much simpler, more pleasant era ... The old sales force must be redesigned to meet the new needs.'

The logic of the strategic sales organization means that new definitions of the sales task will require substantial shifts in the way that the sales organization is managed. Turbulent and ever more complex and demanding markets mandate constant attention to alignment between sales processes and the goals of market and business strategy (Strelsin & Mlot, 1992). However, the evidence suggests that the move from transactional relationships with customers (selling on the basis of price and product advantages) to value-added relationships is proving extremely challenging for many organizations pursuing this strategic direction (*American Salesman*, 2002). Similarly, the shift from individualistic customer relationships to team-based selling around large customers underlines the urgency of new infrastructural requirements in the sales organization (Jones et al., 2005).

Change in the infrastructure supporting the strategic sales organization is likely to span organization structure, performance measurement systems, competency creation systems, and motivation and reward systems – all driven by the definition of the new task and role of the sales operation (Shapiro et al., 1998).

The process of 'reinventing' the sales force to meet the challenges of new markets and new strategies is likely to require attention to several critical issues: focusing on long-term customer relationships, but also assessing customer value and prioritizing the most attractive prospects; creating sales organization structures that are nimble and adaptable to the needs of different customer groups; gaining greater ownership and commitment from salespeople by removing functional barriers within the organization and leveraging team-based working; shifting sales management from 'command and control' to coaching and facilitation; applying new technologies appropriately; designing salesperson evaluation to incorporate the full range of activities and outcomes relevant to new types of sales and account management job (Cravens, 1995).

One recent study of the antecedents and consequences of sales management strategy reveals several issues, which are commonly neglected in leveraging change and superior performance in the sales force and in aligning sales efforts with strategic direction (Baldauf, Cravens, & Piercy, 2005). It should be apparent that new business strategies and an evolving role for the strategic sales organization will inevitably require considerable re-evaluation of the management of the sales organization. There are numerous practical challenges in realigning the selection, training, and development of individuals for these new sales roles (Cron, Marshall, Singh, Spiro, & Sujan, 2005), as well as the development of sales managers with relevant skills and capabilities for the new challenges (Ingram, LaForge, Locander, MacKensie, & Podsakoff, 2005).

Inspiration

Up to this stage the model has been concerned with the routes to the strategic sales organization – getting into the strategy debate, building new, aligned sales processes, and so on. However, there are some broader issues to factor into management thinking as well. We have identified them as inspiration, influence, integrity, and international – but they are linked by the concept of leadership.

One clear implication of a strategic sales organization is that the enhanced role brings with it a responsibility for the executives involved to undertake leadership roles which extend way beyond the traditional confines of the sales force. That leadership will need to provide inspiration, not just feedback and supervision. It will need to be exercised at several levels both within and outside the company. It may be one of the most important challenges that we face in making the strategic sales organization initiative effective.

Indeed, there is growing evidence that leadership questions are given more critical importance in many organizations, operating in the market environments they now face, than ever before. When Sam Palmisano took over as CEO of IBM in 2002, he built a flatter organization with fewer bureaucratic levels, and allocated $100 million to teach his 30,000 managers to lead, not control their staff. (Interestingly, he also asked the board to cut his 2003 bonus and set it aside as a pool of money to be shared by about 20 top executives – worth around $5 million – based on their performance as a team.) He now works with three top teams, each focused on a different aspect of the business and employing the best brains from throughout the company (Ante, 2003).

Indeed, for more than 20 years many of the world's top companies have been 'academy companies' offering intensive leadership training to their executives, because their best young employees are hungry for leadership development. Prime examples are General Electric, Proctor & Gamble, and Nokia. The 'academy company' logic is that competitors can copy every advantage you have got, except one. So, the best companies have realized that their real business is building leaders (Colvin, 2007).

Issues to examine include: leadership within the strategic sales organization – how can senior and middle-ranking executives in the sales organization implement the leadership and followership characteristics relevant to the strategic sales initiative; leadership within the company and the 'top team' responsibilities that come with higher profile – achieving cross-functional and high level influence to support the goals of strategic customer management; leadership in external relationships – playing a key role in the tangled web of relationships common in linking suppliers, collaborators, and customer value; and, leadership in the broader professional business community – winning a seat at the management 'top table' to influence opinion, public policy, and the professional futures of sales and account management.

Influence

Inspiring leadership is important, but leadership has to turn into influence if things are going to be changed. In fact, one of the biggest problems marketing departments have faced in recent years is not so much that they have nothing worth saying, but that they are being ignored when they say it. One potentially disastrous outcome of the low esteem in which many functional specialists appear to hold marketing, is that they stop *listening*. For example, research suggests that when marketers try to share insights and information with other departments, they are frequently ignored or misunderstood – so, often the fight now is actually to get the customer's voice heard in the company (Fazio Maruca, 1998).

Part of the problem is insufficient or weak efforts at communicating with other departments, which is why we see integration and internal marketing as so key to strategizing sales in companies. However, there is more to it. For example, in studying the integration of marketing and R&D, research findings suggest that it is inter-functional rivalry and political pressures that severely reduce R&D's use of information supplied by marketing and sales personnel (Maltz, Souder, & Kumar, 2001). This speaks to declining influence and credibility in contributing to the important debates and decisions within the business. In the absence of formal authority and perhaps weak credibility in some companies, those looking to the strategic sales organization as a force for important change will rely on rebuilding influence within the organization to achieve these goals.

Our view is increasingly that achieving the type of change we have described in strategizing the sales organization, will depend in part on the success of executives in engaging with the rest of the organization and confronting the realities of how it makes important decisions.

Integrity

For the strategic sales organization to fill leadership commitments and exert influence in a company also brings the responsibility for championing integrity – both in dealing with external customers and partner organizations and in working with others in the company. This responsibility brings both some limitations on what actions can be taken, but more importantly is also a source of competitive strength in the marketplace.

Certainly, the level of scrutiny of the ethical standards and corporate social responsibility initiatives undertaken by companies has never been so searching. The attention of pressure groups and the media given to company behaviour is unprecedented, and frequently hostile. The importance is that damage to corporate reputation, however it is brought about, reduces the ability to compete and can undermine the value of a company.

Historically it has been easiest for critics and observers to focus on the selling behaviour of suppliers and much attention has been given to the 'front-end' ethical standards of salespeople and sales management. This continues to be the case. However, the debate has moved on to a much broader ground concerning corporate social responsibility – initiatives to show 'green' or environmental improvements, protecting the working conditions of employees at different stages of the supply chain, reducing the use of scarce resources in the value chain, and so on. This debate has reached a level of maturity now such that it has a substantial impact on buyer–seller relationships and the competitive position of selling organizations. That is the reason why the integrity issue has to feature high on the agenda of any strategic sales organization initiative.

It has been clear for some time that people's judgements of a company's moral standards and corporate responsibility influence whether they want to work for you, whether they want to invest in you, whether they want to supply you, even whether they want to sell for you – but now it is about whether customers want to (or are able to) buy from you.

Many of the most visible and high profile issues of ethics and morality happen at the buyer–seller interface where there is really no place to hide. The test of whether corporate social responsibility initiatives actually enhance customer value happens there too. This underlines the topicality and significance of issues of integrity to the strategic sales organization.

The one thing that is sure is that issues of integrity in seller behaviour and the development of corporate social responsibility initiatives that make business as well as social sense are a high priority for business leaders. Not least among the reasons is the evidence that when major customers are actually asked what they want from sellers, then honesty and integrity top the list (Galea, 2006).

International

It is perhaps stating the obvious to suggest that the strategic sales organization should be shaped in part by an international perspective on customers and management practices. International issues are critical to developing business models and new strategies, to managing the customer portfolio, and to developing the sales organization infrastructure.

In fact, building strong customer relationships is a high priority in most markets wherever they are located, and the strategic sales initiative should play a pivotal role in this activity. At the same time, aggressive globalization and the challenges of gaining a strong competitive edge underline the importance of sales management strategies in gaining competitive advantage in international markets. Increasingly, top managements in many global enterprises are developing their sales force capabilities, recognizing the importance of the sales force in core business processes like customer relationship management, supply chain management, and product development management. Multinational firms like Nestle SA, Novartis, and Caterpillar Inc. have been widely recognized for their successful global sales management systems (Cravens, Piercy, & Low, 2006).

Issues to consider include: why an international perspective is an imperative for the strategic sales organization; how a company can respond to the emergence and rapid growth of global customers who buy on a multinational basis – and the adoption of global account management approaches as an extension of strategic account management; the challenges of global sales management, and particularly the dilemmas about whether to standardize sales management strategy across different countries and cultures, or whether to adapt to local conditions in terms of cultural characteristics, economic wealth, and political stability. The issue is whether international markets are convergent (increasingly the same) or divergent (fundamentally different) – this is not a judgement to be made hastily or incorrectly.

Concluding remarks

The framework we have provided is no more than a tool to identify and address the most urgent issues faced by a company in realigning the way its sales organization is reshaped and reinvented for the new market and customer realities faced. It aims to be flexible enough to accommodate new research findings and insights and specific local issues relevant to a company. At the very least, we hope that the framework provides the basis for recognizing the complexity and cross-functional nature of the process of strategizing the sales organization. We believe that a systematic approach to the organizational issues surrounding the sales organization is more likely to be effective in achieving at least some aspects of transformation.

It was not our intention to develop a set of research propositions. Nonetheless, the framework developed does suggest some interesting opportunities for empirical study. For example, evaluating the configuration of characteristics that are associated with more strategic rather than less strategic sales organizations would be insightful. It would also be useful to investigate the possible interactions between the different variables involved and indeed, whether some play an antecedent role to others. Case-based research into the sales organization transformation process over a period of time would also add greatly to our understanding of the strategizing process.

References

American Salesman. (2002, November). Shift to value-added selling is biggest challenge in sales. *American Salesman*, p. 13.

Ante, S.E. (2003, March 17). The new blue. *Business Week*, pp. 44–50.

Baldauf, A., Cravens, D.W., & Piercy, N. (2005). Sales management control research: Synthesis and an agenda for future research. *Journal of Personal Selling & Sales Management*, 25(1), 7–26.

Chang, J. (2005). From the inside out. *Sales & Marketing Management*, August, 8.

Colvin, G. (2007, October 1). Leader machines. *Fortune*, pp. 60–72.

Cravens, D.W. (1995). The changing role of the sales force. *Marketing Management*, Fall, 17–32.

Cravens, D.W., Piercy, N.F., & Low, G.S. (2006). Globalization of the sales organization: Management control and its consequences. *Organizational Dynamics*, 35(3), 291–303.

Cron, W.L., Marshall, G.W., Singh, J., Spiro, R.L., & Sujan, H. (2005). Salesperson selection, training, and development: Trends, implications, and research opportunities. *Journal of Personal Selling & Sales Management*, 25(2), 123–136.

Deloitte Touche Development. (2005). *Strategic sales compensation survey.* New York: Deloitte Touche Development LLC.

Fazio Maruca, R. (1998). Getting marketing's voice heard. *Harvard Business Review*, January–February, 10–11.

Fink, R.C., Feldman, L.F., & Hatten, K.J. (2007). Supplier performance improvements in relational exchanges. *Journal of Business and Industrial Marketing*, 22(1), 29–40.

Galea, C. (2006). What customers really want. *Sales & Marketing Management*, May, 11–12.

Hamm, S. (2005, April 18). Beyond blue. *Business Week*, pp. 36–42.

Hamm, S. (2008, March 10). Big blue goes for the big win. *Business Week*, pp. 63–65.

HR Chally (2006). *The Chally world class sales excellence research report.* Dayton, OH: The H.R. Chally Group.

Hulbert, J.M., Capon, N., & Piercy, N.F. (2002/2005). *Total integrated marketing: Breaking the bounds of the function*. New York: The Free Press/London: Kogan Page.

IBM. (2005). *The strategic agenda for customer management in the consumer products industry*. New York: IBM Institute for Business Value Executive Brief.

Ingram, T.N., LaForge, B.W., Locander, W.B., MacKensie, S.B., & Podsakoff, P.M. (2005). New directions in sales leadership research. *Journal of Personal Selling & Sales Management*, 25(2), 137–154.

Jones, E., Brown, S.P., Zoltners, A.A., & Weitz, B.A. (2005). The changing environment of selling and sales management. *Journal of Personal Selling & Sales Management*, 25(2), 105–111.

Koerner, L. (2005, February). Conducting an organizational assessment of your SAM programme. Presentation at Strategic Account Management Association Conference, Paris.

Maltz, E., Souder, W.E., & Kumar, A. (2001). Influencing R&D/marketing integration and the use of market information by R&D managers. *Journal of Business Research*, 52(1), 69–82.

Marketing Week. (2003, July 3). Survey reveals 'inadequate' state of internal marketing. *Marketing Week*, p. 8.

McGovern, G.J., Court, D., Quelch, J.A., & Crawford, B. (2004). Bringing customers into the boardroom. *Harvard Business Review*, November, 70–80.

Olson, E.M., Cravens, D.W., & Slater, S.F. (2001). Competitiveness and sales management: A marriage of strategies. *Business Horizons*, March/April, 25–30.

Parker, A., Cohen, N., & Burgess, K. (2009, May 15). BT says sorry as losses spiral. *Financial Times*, p. 15.

Piercy, N.F., & Lane, N. (2009). *Strategic customer management: Strategizing the sales organization*. Oxford: Oxford University Press.

Sales Educators, The. (2006). *Strategic sales leadership: Breakthrough thinking for breakthrough results*. Mason, OH: Thomson.

Seidenschwartz, W. (2005, February). A model for customer enthusiasm: Connecting the customer with internal processes. Presentation at Strategic Account Management Association Conference, Paris.

Shapiro, B.P., Slywotsky, A.J., & Doyle, S.X. (1998). *Strategic sales management: A boardroom issue*. Note 9-595-018. Cambridge, MA: Harvard Business School.

Stephens, H. (2003, August). The H.R. Chally Group. Presentation at the American Marketing Association Summer Educators' Conference, Chicago.

Stewart, T.A. (2006). The top line. *Harvard Business Review*, July–August, 10.

Strelsin, S.C., & Mlot, S. (1992). The art of strategic sales alignment. *Journal of Business Strategy*, 13(6), 41–47.

Tighe, C. (2009, May 9/10). Fear for Teeside as buyers scrap Corus deal. *Financial Times*, p. 4.

Weintraub, A. (2008, February 4). Just say no to drug reps. *Business Week*, p. 69.

Index

intensity 35
internal relationships: competition 113;
lobbying 59–60; marketing 123, 128–9, 131;
partnering 20; transformation 61, 62, 123,
128–9, 131
Internet 120
investment sales personnel 27–8
involvement 123–5

Japan 50–8, 60, 62, 65
Jaramillo, F 74
Jaworski, BJ 104–5, 106, 108
Jones, D 51
Jones, Eli 4
just-in-time production 58–9

key account management 33–45; commitment
34, 35–6, 39, 41–2, 44; control variables 45;
customer equity 5, 34, 36–45; definition of
key accounts 33; intensity and
proactiveness 35; lean enterprise 5–6;
management 34–5, 44–5; market share 42;
marketing 34, 38–9, 53; moderators 45;
performance 5, 33–45; personal
characteristics 34–5; processes 17;
profitability in long-term 41–2; relational
outcomes 33–4; relationship marketing 5,
35–6, 39, 42–3; research 33–6, 43–5;
resources, competition for 44–5; share of
customer spend 41; strategic framework 5,
33–45; theoretical background 34–8;
theoretical model 34, 38–45; trust 34, 35–6,
39, 41–2, 44; value equity 34, 38, 39–40,
42–4
Kinni, T 19
Kirca, AH 16
knowledge of products 58, 60–2
Kohli, AK 104–5, 106, 108
Krachenberg, AR 78

Laforge, Raymond W 4, 5, 19
Lane, Nikala 7, 8, 44, 83, 86
Le Meunier-Fitzhugh, Kenneth 7, 8, 86
leadership 130–1
lean enterprise 5–6, 49–65; accounts,
transparency of 59–60; alignment 6;
background of lean thinking 50–1; bespoke
services, move to 6; competition 60, 64;
culture 62–3; customer interface 56–61, 62–
4; department-company relationships,
changes in 61–2; education and
information 58, 60–3; expectations of
customers 59–60; International Motor
Vehicle Programme 50–1; Japan 50–8, 60,
62, 65; key account management 5–6; long-
term customer relationships 53, 64–5;
market orientation 62–4; marketing 62–3;

metrics 54, 59–60; motor sector 50–4, 60,
62, 64–5; open book costing 57; order
management 58–9; price 57, 64; process-
based approach 50; products 57–8, 60, 61–
2; research 53–5; sales force transformation
6, 52–64; service provision 58; spread of
lean approaches 51–3; standards, adoption
of 59; supplier relationships 49–56, 59;
traditional approaches, move away from 6;
transformation 6, 51, 54–6, 61–4;
transparency 5; trickle-down effect 52;
working practices, changes in 6
Leigh, TW 86
Lemon, KM 38, 42, 44
levels, reduction in organizational 16–17
Lincoln, YS 88
Loken, B 74
lone wolf tendencies 74, 79
loyalty programs 37–8
Lyons, TE 78

Madoff Ponzi scheme 76
Malshe, Avinash 7–8
market intelligence/information: collaboration
104, 107–8, 111–13; competition 126; lean
enterprise 63; market orientation 108, 113;
marketing and sales relationships 27, 84,
86, 95, 98, 104, 107–8, 111–13; research
and development 131; sources of data 104;
transformation 123, 124, 126, 131
market orientation (MO) 9, 15–16: adaptive
selling 19; alignment 15–16, 19;
collaboration 7, 103–15; coordination 113–
14; cross-functional cooperation 16; culture
15; customer-oriented selling 19; customer-
value agents 19; ethics 69–70, 80; lean
enterprise 62–4; market intelligence/
information 7, 103–15; marketing and sales
relationships 7, 95, 103–15; performance 7,
15–16, 103–15; processes 15, 17; sales force
69; superior customer value 15–16;
transformation 15–16, 19; value, definition
of 19
marketing and sales relationships 83–99:
alignment 17–18, 22–4, 27; B2B 7, 103–15;
channels, use of multiple 22; collaboration
7, 27, 85, 103–15; competition 113–14;
competition between internal groups 113;
conceptual development 104–8; conflicts
18, 27, 84–5, 107, 113; coordination 18, 85,
106–7, 111, 113–14; cross-functionality 22,
111, 113; culture 106–7, 113; customer
relationship management 86, 91–2, 95–9,
114; decision-making 89, 95, 98, 114;
executives: challenges 96, 97, perceptions of
roles of 7, 95–6; facilitators 84, 93–5, 97;
independence of sales force 27; interface